THE BLACK ROSE

THE BLACK ROSE

My Story of Colourism Silently Lived by Millions

Written by
Shweta Aggarwal

First published in Great Britain in 2022 by Curious Minds Press Ltd

Copyright © Curious Minds Press Ltd

The moral right of the author has been asserted

First Edition.

ISBN: 978-0-9932328-7-9

In loving memory of my dearest Papa.

Author's Note

The events described in this memoir are based on my life experiences. Others involved in these experiences may recall the incidents differently. This is my truth. My observations and the views shared here about my journey through colourism are not intended to offend anyone.

Most names are pseudonyms to protect the identities of those individuals. For the same reason, I have refrained from describing certain characters in depth.

Any resemblance to persons living or dead resulting from changes to names is entirely coincidental and unintentional.

TABLE OF CONTENTS

*"People will forget what you said,
people will forget what you did,
but people will never forget how you made them feel."*

Maya Angelou

PROLOGUE

Ever wondered what effect persistent bullying has on a six-year-old? Ask a forty-five-year-old. Ask me.

Ever since the Black Lives Matter movement following the brutal murder of George Floyd in 2020, I have found myself sharing numerous stories about my past with my two children and husband. Having experienced colour prejudice or insensitive remarks about my brown skin tone throughout my life, my past has come back to haunt me . . . uninvited and unwanted. A 'dark' past. Or as Indians would call it, a 'kala' past.

Although I have mostly had a wonderful, blessed life, growing up between India and Japan, and now living in the UK, there are elements of my past that are painful, to say the least. Painful because I happened to be born dark-skinned to fair parents. And this was seen by some Indians as an open invitation for taunting and derogatory comments.

For hundreds of years, Indians have harboured the notion that being fair-skinned is a ticket to superiority. That's right – white supremacy doesn't just exist among white people. Sadly, this is still the case even in modern, 'liberated' India.

For years I have tried to forget my painful past, like childbirth. But the remarks, even now, are relentless, leaving me festering like a sore. Writing about my past is an attempt to face this colour prejudice head-on.

They say writers should write what they know. I am not a writer. My memoir is about who I was and who I have become. As it is a collage of extracts from my memory, digging deep from the tender age of six, the rendition is not as clear-cut as black and white. There are several shades of brown in between, no pun intended! Unravelling my story, I discovered more than I was prepared for: many buried secrets, some darker than colourism.

1
TIPPING POINT

May 2020, England

Colourism. It's complicated. There are blurred lines, or perhaps 'blurred shades' would be more appropriate. So, allow me to start with its dictionary definition.

colourism

(US colorism)

Pronunciation /ˈkʌlərɪz(ə)m/

NOUN

abstract noun

Prejudice or discrimination against individuals with a dark skin tone, typically among people of the same ethnic or racial group.

The term is believed to be first coined by author Alice Walker in 1982 and added to the Oxford Dictionary in June 2015.[1] Let me draw your attention to a key phrase in the definition: 'typically among people of the *same* ethnic or racial group.'

Those with darker skin experience prejudice or discrimination while fair-skinned individuals enjoy a form of white supremacy: white skin privilege. Where I come from, India, the belief that 'fair is beautiful' is an omnipresent notion, implicit in every household. Without your knowledge, your colour is discussed in the family even before you're born. Yes, in India, a country predominantly populated with various shades of brown. And it doesn't stop at standards of beauty. Certain privileges are also granted to fairer-skinned people, such as careers in the media.

When I first experienced colourism in India back in the 1980s, the belief wasn't defined by this one word. I was introduced to it through four words that became a part of my vocabulary before I had even learned to read and write full sentences.

1. *Gora (masculine) / Gori (feminine)* – fair or white (highly desirable)

2. *Ghehuan* (gender neutral) – 'wheatish' complexion

3. *Saanvla / Saanvli* – bronze or brown skin tone

4. *Kala / Kali* – very dark skin tone (black)

This fairness barometer, a 'Fairometer', was used to grade everyone's skin tone. It still is. I thought I was a genius for coming up with this term until I came across a profile on Twitter that promoted a website to grade one's skin tone. Thank goodness the website is now inactive. Google also listed an article by Bhargavi Agrawal, titled *The Fairometer of Beauty*, which discussed how the words *fair* and *beautiful* are used interchangeably in India. The four words above are how *I* define the Fairometer.

These four words are used casually among Indians to describe people based on their skin tone, often without considering any emotional repercussions. Even in 2022, this Fairometer still drives 'colour conversations' in which home 'remedies' are discussed to lighten skin tone, and cosmetic products are manufactured to help people climb the ranks. Defining skin tones for shades of matching make-up is one thing. Defining beauty based on colour is another. Alas, the definition of beauty in India is crude and unforgiving.

Taunted for my colour ever since I can remember, I too started believing the world and the people in it would appear more beautiful if seen through white-tinted glasses. And so began my journey of complexes and confusion, which eventually led to me surrendering to colourism. Until now, at age forty-five.

Everyone has a tipping point; the moment at which they can take no more. The last drop in their vessel of tolerance before it overspills. George Floyd's murder on 25 May 2020 in Minnesota, US was the last drop in my vessel. Floyd, a black American, was brutally suffocated in the custody of a white police officer, Derek Chauvin. Handcuffed and pinned to the ground under Chauvin's knee for several minutes, Floyd's last words were, 'I can't breathe.' He was killed simply for being reported for using a counterfeit $20 bill. Chauvin was convicted of Floyd's murder a year later.[2]

The Black Lives Matter movement, which triggered global protests, filled me with a deeply unsettling feeling. I couldn't sleep for days. Everywhere I went, I felt as if I were the only culprit in the entire universe, as if every fluttering leaf, the wind, the birds, and the streams, were urging me to come clean. The sun during the day, the moon and stars at night – all shining their light on me to expose my behaviour. I felt shallow because of my guilt. But I have never knowingly discriminated against black people, so why did guilt embed itself in my subconscious?

It's because colourism is a cousin of racism, their common grandparent being white supremacy. I realised that by wishing to be fairer, I wasn't just succumbing to colourism, I was validating white skin privilege and subsequently, white supremacy. As someone who has experienced decades of bullying for her dark skin tone, the realisation of this hypocrisy became the catalyst for penning this memoir.

Many great writers I have learned from say, 'You know when you have a story to write and when you must write it.' My story had been sleeping in my subconscious for several years. It woke up during the Black Lives Matter protests, took charge, and since then, I have merely been a puppet with a pen. When I started to dig deeper, peeling off the layers of baggage I'd accumulated over the years, I realised a family holiday in Thailand in 2016 was when the idea for my book first stirred. It was the first missed opportunity to write, to instigate change, both in colourism and within myself. So, allow me to begin from the beginning: the very first glimpse of guilt and undeniable hypocrisy, buried for way too long.

2

HYPOCRISY HURTS

July 2016, Thailand

A magnetic pull drew me closer to an item for which I had a strong radar. We go back a long way. Bright white lights enhanced its glow, luring me into submission. Of all the places in the world, I did not expect to see it in Bangkok Airport's duty-free shops. I walked closer to the item and further away from my family.

I don't normally have the patience to meander through Arrivals. And enduring a twelve-hour flight from London Heathrow with my eight-year-old son, Rohan, and nine-year-old daughter, Kareena, should have been a good enough reason to want to escape the airport swiftly.

'What is it, Mummy? Can we go now?' asked Kareena, curious and restless at the same time.

'Coming, darling.' I hurried over to join them.

The soporific taxi ride to our hotel through heavy traffic had everyone dozing off within minutes. Except me. I still couldn't get my head around what I had seen in duty-free – a skin-whitening cream. This product and I had a long history, but this was the first time I had seen it outside of India.

Check-in at the hotel was slow, and we were all starving. We asked the receptionist to store our luggage somewhere safe and rushed out in search of the nearest Thai restaurant. Luckily, we found a quaint restaurant a stone's throw away. We didn't bother reading the menu on the window, went straight in, and came out just over thirty minutes later. Walking back to the hotel, I saw a cosmetics store that had the same whitening cream on display. I stopped again.

Why do I keep coming across this?

It was almost as if it was a sign. It was, but I didn't know then that it was an ominous one. I was about to face some very uncomfortable truths.

The walk woke us all up, as did the idea of jumping into the pool as soon as my husband, Amit, suggested it. Kareena and Rohan slipped into their swimsuits and slippers quickly. I lathered them up with sunblock and told Amit I'd join them shortly. The moment they left the room, I searched for my special cream. I rummaged through my entire suitcase twice but couldn't find it. For most people spending a whole day in the sunshine, SPF alone is enough, given that their primary aim is to protect their skin from sun damage. I would do the same with my whitening cream first, followed by sunblock. I believed the two layers yielded better protection, my primary aim being to protect my colour.

My cream and I were inseparable on beach holidays, but that day, I could picture the tube of cream in my bathroom cabinet in London, looking very lonesome. I used to keep it hidden behind sanitary pads. My relationship with this cream could be described in one word: masochistic. It played on my insecurities with the image of the lady on the tube displayed in four different shades from *kali* to *gori*. An explicit message that *only* 'fair is beautiful'. The Fairometer bragging. This cream was also my only confidant. The only thing that was aware of my insecurities. The only thing that had been by my side for decades.

When I turned up by the poolside, Kareena and Rohan were surprised to see me in my exercise leggings, T-shirt, and trainers.

'Aren't you going to swim with us, Mummy?' they asked.

'How about you both enjoy some time with Daddy?' I sneaked to the gym overlooking the pool and watched my family splashing around, making memories.

With our second wave of energy in the evening, we stepped off the taxi boat onto Bangkok's riverfront market. Asiatique, a concrete oasis for restaurant lovers, shopaholics and funfair junkies, was a burst of all things Thailand under one roof. After dinner, we wandered through the walkways full of street stalls. T-shirts, jewellery, fake sports goods, bikinis . . . and skin-whitening creams. I stopped for the third time. I couldn't understand why the locals in Thailand used it. To me, they had nothing to worry about. Their complexion was a warm blend of white and bronze, highly sought after in the Western world and between *gora* and *ghehuan* on the Indian Fairometer. Yet the cream was present everywhere, rubbed in your face from the moment you got off the plane. Observing their desire for fairer skin, I learned that complexion-related insecurities prevailed in Thailand too. But I was more concerned about my own for now.

'Hey sweetie, I'll catch up with you in a few minutes. Can you take the kids with you? Your phone is switched on, right?' I turned straight to the stall without waiting for Amit's reply. The whitening cream had my undivided attention.

'Excuse me,' I said to the lady running the stall. 'Can you tell me a little more about this cream? How strong is it? What's special about the snail extract? How does it help?' I bombarded her with my questions. Before the lady could reply, I heard Kareena rustling behind me.

'What is this, Mummy?' she asked.

'What are you doing here? You should be with Daddy!' I immediately rang Amit to inform him.

'I wanted to be with you. Why are you buying a skin-whitening cream, Mummy?' She glanced at the tubs of cream stacked on the table.

A very long silence followed. Or at least it did from my end. Kareena, on the other hand, kept asking the question like she was on repeat play. A precocious child, she had started talking at ten months, could recite my 11-digit mobile number by the time she was one, and had learned the alphabet and numbers up to 20 by eighteen months. She reasoned with astounding logic even as a toddler.

As a parent, there have been numerous occasions where I have had to invent answers to awkward questions. I had mastered the art just as well as reading the 'give me the truth' look in Kareena's eyes. She held that look today. Her question knocked on the door of my private, insecure world that not even Amit was privy to. I had never imagined that it would be exposed one day, especially to my children. I braced myself for what felt like an interrogation. Although I could predict her questions, I was tongue-tied. I wasn't willing to tell the whole truth either. Losing my composure, I responded inadequately.

'It makes your skin fairer,' I said.

'Why do you want to be fairer?'

There it was, the second dreaded question. Then came the final blow.

'Aren't you happy with your skin colour? You tell us to be happy with who we are.'

Tired, exposed, and emotional, I wasn't as brave as I was hoping to be, so I chose deflection. 'It's getting late. We should find Daddy and go back to the hotel.'

I didn't purchase the cream and hoped that by the next morning Kareena would have forgotten the conversation. I had trouble falling asleep that night. I had never dodged her questions, no matter how difficult the subject matter. It was our family's mantra that the children should always discuss anything on their minds and we as parents would always answer them and close the issue. The entire conversation had gone horribly wrong. I sensed that she saw right through me and that there were more questions coming. But she kept me waiting. She asked me when I least expected it.

Two days later, we caught an early morning flight from Bangkok to Koh Samui. By 4 p.m., we were settled in at Amari Beach Resort. While Amit and Rohan were playing catch in the pool, Kareena and I were reading on our sunbeds. I shifted the position of my sunbed every time a ray of the sun touched my skin. Kareena, in an aqua blue swimsuit, was enjoying basking in the sun. To my left, a middle-aged English couple were topping up their tanning oil. This was the third time I had seen them reapply it. I smiled at them and engaged in a quick holiday conversation, glancing at their bottle a couple of times. A skin-whitening cream in a brown person's beach bag and a tanning oil in the hands of a white person. The epitome of irony.

When I turned back towards Kareena, I saw an Indian family strolling towards the sunbeds adjacent to hers. They too were a family of four, with a boy and a girl, both younger than my children. And they were loud, like me. It was evident that the mother did not intend to jump into the pool; she was fully clothed in everything but swimwear. Her children wore full-length swimsuits and floppy, oversized hats. I watched her smear sunblock over the only body parts left exposed – hands, feet, and face. She instructed her husband, 'No more than an hour. They must come out then.' She didn't join her family.

Exactly one hour later, as though the lady had set an alarm, she returned to get her family out of the pool. Her children's pleas for more time made no difference.

'So many children are still playing in the pool, Mummy,' they observed. 'Why can't we play?'

'You'll turn *kala*,' she replied. 'Come out now.' Her children sat on their sunbeds, slurping their milkshakes. Enviously, they watched the pool full of other children playing.

'Outrageous!' I said, agitated, placing my book on my lap.

'Why, Mummy?' Kareena asked.

'Because she's denying her children a fun holiday to prevent them from tanning. They shouldn't be here on a beach holiday if that's her main concern.'

'You're here on a beach holiday and you're afraid of tanning.'

'Yes. But *they* don't need to worry about tanning. They are very fair.' I regretted the words as soon as I blurted them out.

'You shouldn't be worrying about it either. You're not happy with your colour when you tell *us* to be happy with who *we* are. I saw you buying the cream at Bangkok airport before we caught the flight to Koh Samui.'

Damn it! I had been purchasing these creams for decades without arousing a hint of suspicion. All it took was one pair of young inquisitive eyes to bust me.

'What's the difference between you and them?' my daughter asked. 'They are trying to preserve their colour by staying out of the sun, and you're trying to change your colour by using creams.'

She was right. I had no right to judge the actions of others while I was still obsessed with my colour. Who was I to decide that I had a greater right to strive for fairness than that lady? I had become what I had been fighting against my entire life. At that moment, Kareena's eyes were a mirror reflecting a disgraceful version of me: a hypocritical mother who spent her day preaching good values to her children but didn't live up to those values in her own life.

I didn't see my little nine-year-old girl in front of me. I saw someone who had caught me red-handed, living the biggest lie of my life. I saw someone who, up until that day, had me on a pedestal. My heart and stomach sank in unison, knowing that this conversation had knocked me off that pedestal. I felt smaller than Kareena.

How do I redeem myself with her and, more importantly, myself?

The only way to earn my way back onto the pedestal was by telling the truth. But facing a disappointed child required more courage than I had ever imagined. And I needed time to gather that sort of courage.

'It's not so simple,' I said. Kareena wasn't satisfied with my response. In a child's world, everything is simple, without nuance. She held me in an unforgiving stare.

'It's a long story.' I tried to evade my confession one last time.

'Can I have an ice cream then?' she said. I could see she wasn't going to let this go.

'You might need more than one,' I smiled, doting on her innocence. I ordered a chocolate ice cream for Kareena and a piña colada for myself from the poolside waiter.

Of course, I should have been practising what I preached. However, banishing complexes that had been ingrained in me from a very young age was easier said than done. After years of being bullied for my colour, I was still succumbing to the bullies by purchasing whitening creams. It had become innate behaviour.

Kareena may not understand my story, but I decided to share everything. Our roles had reversed. As parents, we tell our children to always own up to any wrongdoings; they may be rebuked, but we will be there to listen and solve problems. At that moment, Kareena was a nine-year-old mother, and I was a thirty-nine-year-old girl, owning up to my misdemeanours, hoping she would be sympathetic.

I also hoped that in this case, my vulnerability might prove to be a strength and a blessing in disguise. By confiding in my daughter, I was laying down the ground rules even thicker: that she must do the same when the need arises.

This was going to be her first lesson that not everything in life is clear-cut. For the lesson to be fruitful, narrating my story unfiltered and from the very beginning was the only option. After all, complexes are rarely the result of just one upsetting incident or a single insecurity. There are always more layers than meets the eye. Indelible memories of my early childhood days at boarding school played in my head, tormenting me. I started welling up, but I knew that this was the moment to share everything. Besides, the pool seemed like the right setting for the coming waterworks.

3

A BAD DREAM

February 1984, India

Tears gushed down my cheeks. I was choking on a throbbing lump in my throat. My heart was competing with the lump, beating faster and louder, every deafening thump pounding behind my eardrums. The only other time I have felt this way was when I lost my father to lung cancer in 2009. He was fifty-six, and I was thirty-two.

But this was 1984, and I was six.

'I promise I'll be good. Please take me with you. Please don't leave me here. Papa, please.' I sobbed and begged, clinging to my father's leg. My grip was tight, and for a moment, I thought I must have been hurting him.

'It's only for a short while. I'll come and get you very soon,' Papa said, squatting to comfort me one more time with a hug.

I had just been enrolled in a boarding school, convinced that I was being punished for a crime I had unknowingly committed. As I scanned my memory, images flashed across my eyes like a camera reel – blurry, black-and-white sketches of everything mischievous I had ever done that could be categorised as a criminal offence. One memory stuck out from a few months previously . . .

It was a hot Sunday afternoon, curtains drawn to keep the bedroom cool; the sun rays peering in were playing hide and seek in between the pleats. We didn't own an air conditioner or a cooler, a real luxury in the scorching heat of Rajasthan. Our humble, one-bedroom bungalow in Vigyan Nagar, a small housing-board colony, was one of many identical bungalows. Papa had just woken up from his routine Sunday nap and stumbled to the toilet. He had heavy feet, which is how I knew he had left the bedroom. I had been observing him for days; his habit of smoking before naps intrigued me. He looked relaxed when smoking. The magical puffs of smoke attracted me to cigarettes, how with every breath he exhaled, the clouds would float and dissipate gracefully, as though dancing their way out in slow motion. Perhaps, ironically, it was *this* smoke that ignited a passion for dance that would continue throughout my life.

I entered the bedroom, as quiet as a mouse, and found an inviting cigarette stub on the cold stone inlay floor. It was still lit, a few faint red embers further sparking my curiosity. I picked it up between my two forefingers, like Papa did, rounded my lips to create a cavity for the stub, and inhaled hard. I thought I could take a deep drag like Papa and breathe out the smoke in one smooth operation. To my surprise, I coughed violently instead.

Papa came running in to find me spluttering on the floor. I will never forget the rage in his eyes, contrary to his usually calm disposition. I will also never forget the imprint of his entire right hand on my left cheek. Despite expressing his anger in the form of a slap, his fury still had him shaking.

'NEVER touch this or any cigarette again!' he yelled. 'You understand? It's *really* bad for you.'

I didn't recognise the man towering over me. He could not have been my Papa. My father was a man who never tired of reading my favourite bedtime story, *The Lion and the Hare*, every night because it brought me joy. My father would carry me around all day, even to the toilet, because I craved his attention constantly. He would buy me my favourite chocolate bar, Five Star, at the end of every month even if I forgot to remind him. He never slapped me. And if this was my father, glaring at me, smoking must have been an unforgivable crime. Shocked by seeing this side of him, I dared not ask why he smoked a dozen cigarettes a day if it was so 'bad' for you. To this day, I have not touched a cigarette. The slap worked.

That must have been it. The crime. The cigarette must have been the reason why my father was sending me to this boarding school.

'Papa, I will never touch a cigarette again. Never! Please don't leave me here,' I wailed.

'It's not that, *beta*. You'll be here only for a few months. I'll come and get you very soon.' He said a few more things, but I had zoned out by then, unable to understand anything. Noticing my absent mental state, Papa stood up, the hint of a tear sparkling in his eyes. I moved my arms from around his neck and wrapped them around his right leg, clinging to him determinedly.

The matron of the boarding school stood by, witnessing all this as a silent spectator. She stepped closer, unwrapped my arms, and signalled for Papa to leave. Then, she grabbed my hand to escort me to my room. I don't remember Papa turning around to catch a glimpse; he must have been hiding his tears. February 1984 (the exact date doesn't come to mind), I was declared an official resident of this prison.

Name: Shweta Khandelwal

Age: 6 years and 5 months

Offence: Smoking?

Punishment: Imprisonment in Virendra Gram Boarding School, Haryana, for 'a few months'

Down a few stairs from the main office building and straight ahead, I took my first step towards my cell. It wasn't a long walk. The matron turned left and there it was – a large semi-circular structure with Rooms 1–15 for girls and 16–30 for boys. Outside the rooms lay a vast, empty field for sporting activities. Kareena's first school had a similar semi-circular structure for classrooms. Life always has a way of coming around in a semi-circle!

I stood by the doorway of the dorm room, my feet as heavy as sandbags, my grip on the matron's hand tight. She yanked me in. 'This is Payal, Rohit, and Sheetal,' she said, pointing at three children. 'And this is your bed.'

That was it. She left.

I studied each one of them through my teary eyes. Sheetal was pretty. Her brown, shoulder-length hair, dark brown eyes, petite frame, and olive skin, all drew me to her immediately. When I think about her now, I realise she looked European. She also happened to be the only one who smiled. Payal and Rohit didn't acknowledge me. I felt indifferent towards Rohit, coy and insipid. But Payal's aura screamed arrogance. She was a teenager, tall, and boasted a heavier, sportier frame than Sheetal. The facial features of all three bore an uncanny resemblance to one another. At first, I thought it was my distorted vision. Then, I learned that they were in fact siblings.

I also learned that our room enjoyed some exceptions to the boarding school rules. Children in a similar age bracket usually shared rooms, but Payal and Rohit were a few years older than Sheetal and me. Rooms were also meant to be single-sex, yet Rohit – a boy – was another exception to the rule. They must have belonged to a powerful family. Not rich as such, but influential. Perhaps some civil-service connection. In India, where there was a will to bend the rules, there was always a way. Three siblings and lucky me in Room 11.

My rickety, metal-frame bed was on the right side of the room, at the far end. The bathroom was next door, adjacent to my damp, chipped wall. I started to unpack clothes from my *sandook,* an aluminium trunk, stacking them on the shelves directly above the bed. Sheetal came over, but I wasn't ready to talk to her yet. She sensed my tense body language and returned to her bed.

Although it was only mid-afternoon, and there was a mountain of a day to get through, I don't remember anything else that happened until bedtime. *Why am I here?* I tried hard to remember what Papa had said but couldn't recollect a word.

The next morning, I struggled to open my swollen eyelids. Beneath them, my eyes were dry and tight. I rubbed them ruthlessly, but they weren't ready to cooperate. Besides, another sensation required my attention urgently. My back was soaking wet. I lay drenched in a warm, soggy sheet.

Have I cried my eyes dry and my bed wet?

Sight is usually the first sense we associate with being awake. My eyes were still closed, but I was wide awake, courtesy of a pungent smell. I dragged myself out, squinting, and stared at the large wet patch on my sheet. A puddle of urine was staring back at me. This was a familiar sensation but in an unfamiliar setting. I looked around and realised I wasn't at home. This was my very first night away from home, from my bed, from my comfort blanket – my Mummy.

Back home, when I used to wet my bed, Mummy took care of it all, from changing me to changing and washing the sheets. We didn't have a washing machine; she hand-washed all our laundry, including sheets, but it never occurred to me how cumbersome it was for her. Every night she made sure I visited the toilet before tucking me in. Then she woke me up in the middle of the night for a second visit in my semi-conscious state. Despite that, I still managed to reward her with a soggy sheet most mornings, yet she never complained.

I continued to stare at the wet patch, without a clue as to what to do. Then I remembered Mummy had packed a wax cloth, which she had instructed me to put between the mattress and the sheet.

'Don't forget to put this on or else the mattress will take a long time to dry out and the smell will linger,' she had said.

I panicked and flung open the trunk lid. There lay the wax cloth. Having battled single-handedly through the longest day of my life, I must have collapsed onto the bed, forgetting it. I pulled the sheet as hard as I could and discovered a larger wet patch on the mattress. Before anyone could catch a whiff, I picked up the four corners of the sheet, gathered it in one messy bundle, and rushed towards the bathroom, tripping over a few times. Too late. Payal was up. 'Gross! Did you pee in your bed? What are you, a baby?' she yelled. Rohit was stirring, and Sheetal sat up. Her sympathetic stare was comforting, almost hypnotic; it gave me the courage to speak up.

'I had a bad dream,' I lied. I stood frozen, soaked in warm urine. How I wished that my admittance to the boarding school was a bad dream, that Mummy would wake me up and walk me to the toilet, that I would find myself in the comfort of my own bed, familiar with every contour of my body, that I would feel Mummy's body warmth as I curled into her cushiony arm.

I replayed Payal's words in my mind: 'Are you a baby?'

'This is my crime,' I mumbled under my breath.

I am a six-year-old baby who wets her bed almost every night. This is why Mummy and Papa thought I would be better off at a boarding school. Mummy had had enough of washing up after me.

Bedwetting was not an occasional mishap triggered by bad dreams. It was one of my realities, part of my identity. In fact, it was the very first of many monikers beginning with a capital 'B' in my life – Bedwetter. In my conscious state, Mummy said I was an obedient and intelligent child. She said I learned to talk and walk when I was ten months old. For my school interview, I chose to dance on the headmistress' desk when she asked what I enjoyed most. To my parents' surprise, the school offered me a place. The headmistress said my confidence impressed her. Conscious choices of a confident child. But come night-time, trying to conquer bedwetting in an unconscious state was no child's play. Every night, I would whisper to myself, 'Be good. Hold it in.' But my bladder would disobey. Every morning it disappointed me, and I, in turn, disappointed my mother. It was like I had two equal and opposite versions of myself, as different as day and night. My confidence shattered every morning, and I spent the rest of the day picking up the pieces by being sickeningly obedient. Being a goody-two-shoes meant I never gave Mummy the chance to be ashamed of anything else about me.

Back then, we couldn't afford special night nappies either. Unnecessary laundry became a part of Mummy's daily ritual, and I was oblivious to her grimacing. I had heard her and Papa talk about it occasionally, but they would brush it off if I asked any questions. 'It happens to a lot of kids,' they would say. 'It'll fix itself.'

The boarding school must be for children who wet their beds, a place where they come to get 'fixed'. I glanced at the other three beds.

'What are you looking at?' barked Payal.

Three crisp, dry sheets and three confident faces.

Turned out, I was the only one in the entire boarding school with this condition. Word of the mattress hanging out to dry spread like wildfire. Within a few days, the entire boarding school was familiar with my situation. Within a few days, I was washing my own sheets. Every day.

4

HOME

February 1984, India

I don't remember how many days it took for me to step out of my dark, collapsing world. I wandered the school campus as though blindfolded with a meshy material that gave a hazy view of the prison. But then one day, Sheetal saved a seat for me in class. As I sat down next to her on the bench, she whispered, 'Do you know what we call the matron?' Knowing it was a rhetorical question, I waited for her to carry on.

'Humpty Dumpty,' she chuckled.

I giggled. That nickname was spot-on for her! As slender as her arms were, her body was large and spherical around her waist and hips. I tried to call her Humpty Dumpty in my head, but even in my head, I refrained. I shifted closer to Sheetal and nestled into the bench. The blindfolds came off that day, the first time I took notice of my new surroundings.

Virendra Gram Boarding School in Haryana, Delhi's neighbouring state, stretched over acres of land. The drive there, down a long, single-lane road, seemed to go on for eternity. In fact, it was barely a road. It was dusty, filled with potholes, and cut through desolate landscape on either side with rare sightings of greenery.

The black, wrought-iron entrance gates were on the left side of the road. Within the premises, the boarding school did not fail to impress. Although secluded, it had every facility you could think of and more, for the 1980s. To me, it was still a glorified prison. After all, prisons are also usually secluded, keeping their prisoners at a distance from all the law-abiding citizens.

There was a basketball court and a roller-skating track on the left, a garden and a swimming pool on the right. Well, it was merely an enormous tank filled with water, not like anything you're imagining – no shimmering blue pool with lanes and sunbeds. This pool was green from the algae at the bottom and too deep to stand in, yet it was the highlight of our weekly schedule. The main office building further up on the right had a canteen and an indoor play area with two table-tennis tables. I don't remember much more than that.

I settled in eventually. Misery turned into endurance, and tears ever-ready to shed learned self-control. However, I still cried inconsolably every time my parents called. Because I had to take the calls in the matron's office, I was unable to have a heart-to-heart in her presence. How was I to tell my parents I hated every minute of it here? I would hold it all in and weep the moment I set foot outside the office.

Sheetal would pacify me in our room. In her, I had found my anchor. She was intelligent, sporty, and kind enough to take me under her wing. While Payal took great pleasure in reducing me to tears every day, Sheetal offered a shoulder to cry on. Payal wasn't particularly nice to her siblings either. Perhaps she saw me as her sibling too, the one she disliked most and made the target of most of her abuse. I never retaliated and responded only with silence.

'That stinks!'

'Oh my God, I'm going to vomit!'

'This is why your parents have left you here.'

'*Susu* Shweta' (Pee Shweta)

These were just some of Payal's daily insults. A popular playground name-calling game was to rhyme colours with insulting remarks.

Yellow, yellow, dirty fellow.

Pink, pink, you stink.

Blue, blue, your chaddi (underwear) flew.

Red, red, susu in your bed.

At that last line, everyone used to look over at me and snigger.

After a while, I couldn't work out whether the bed-wetting was an uncontrollable bodily impulse or whether it happened in response to Payal's daily taunts. Was it because of the anxiety from being bullied? Was it the feeling of despair at being away from family? Were bad dreams to blame? Or was it simply a self-fulfilling prophecy? Payal would start the day showering me with unprovoked comments. Then at night, as if to hand her a victory again, I would wet my bed.

Whatever it was, almost every morning at around the same time – 4:00 a.m. – I lay in my bed with a soggy nightie and sheet, contemplating how to get up without waking up the others. If I made it to the bathroom, I would stand there wondering whether I had enough time to wash my sheet or if I should do it after all the morning activities. Shoving the sheet into the bucket and giving it a quick stir was easy. Pulling it out again, my arms burned like I was drawing water from a well. Wringing and hanging the sheet was the most challenging part; the line was out of my reach, even on my tippy toes. I still remember the weight of the drenched sheet on my shoulders and the arduous ritual it was for my small body.

I probably did have some bad dreams. It's hard enough remembering your real experiences from the age of six, recollecting dreams or nightmares is a whole different challenge. One of my daydreams is crystal clear, though - escaping from the prison and out of the black gates for good. When fatigued by the bedwetting ritual, I would lie in bed, staring at the ceiling, searching for answers to one question: *Why am I here?* I was never sure of the answers, guesses really. So, I enjoyed my virtual escapades instead in which I would run all the way to the house of my Nani, my maternal grandmother, in Delhi, more than 20 km away. Or I would hitchhike, hoping some Good Samaritan would be kind enough to drop a six-year-old home.

The daydreams always ended abruptly. I would be hiding in the garden by the black gates, waiting for a vehicle to approach. The gates would swing open, and I would sneak out to freedom. Then the bell would ring at 5 a.m. sharp.

Fifteen minutes. That's all we had to get ready in the mornings. At exactly 5.15 a.m., we were summoned to the field opposite our rooms. Changing my sheet and nightie, having a quick flannel wash, listening to Payal bark, bossing us all around, and sometimes having to change in front of Rohit – all of this was another ritual.

Then began each morning's incessant activities: shooting (yes, shooting with rifles), field games, a jog to the basketball court, followed by a match. As I was never picked to play, I usually sat on a bench by the court, close to the black gates, daydreaming again. Sometimes, I would plan to sneak out in the middle of a game. It was an extremely ambitious plan. Downright foolish, in fact. So instead, I would wait for the breakfast bell at 7.30 a.m. It wasn't like I had a spread of scrumptious breakfast goodies waiting for me in the canteen. I can still taste an overdone, dry, boiled egg in my mouth, which we had to eat every day. Like the cigarette, I've never touched a boiled egg again either.

I looked forward to dinner as much as I hated breakfast. This was where I was introduced to chicken. Sheetal suggested I try it once, and I devoured everything on my plate. Although I was a Hindu, from that day on, chicken became my solace. In every prison, to survive, you have to find the one thing that keeps you going. Chicken curry was my one thing, served once a week for dinner. Despite being the scrawniest in my class, I had a big appetite, especially for chicken.

I wasn't the sporty kind either. It's funny how my daydreams consisted of running away when I used to sprain my ankle often, sometimes when running to the matron's office for a phone call from my parents, sometimes conveniently timed to miss a lesson. I would end up with my foot soaking in a bucket of hot water and salt.

One such afternoon I was sitting on my bed, leaning over the footbath, letting my tears drop into the bucket, when Sheetal entered, laughing uncontrollably. She held her stomach, struggling to catch her breath.

'What's wrong?' she asked, taking a few moments to

compose herself. 'Phone call again?'

'Papa said this is the last time he'll be able to call here. The matron won't allow it anymore. She told Papa I have settled in and that they don't need to speak to me so often.'

'Oh,' Sheetal moved closer to sit beside me. 'How will you be able to speak to them?'

'At my Nani's house, once every two weeks,' I sobbed. 'Just twice a month!'

Sheetal always cheered me up. Like when I fell during a three-legged race and grazed both knees. I wanted Mummy, but Sheetal comforted me instead. Like when I grew tired while washing my sheet, crying by the bathroom tap. Sheetal helped me. Later, Payal told her off. Like the time a teacher punished me for not using my right hand to write. All the teachers were adamant that I switch hands but never explained why it was necessary. One day, a teacher twisted my right ear, ordered me to put my right hand out on my desk, and slapped my knuckles with the sharp edge of a ruler. I switched to being right-handed for life. That day, at recess, Sheetal wrapped a handkerchief around my bleeding knuckle. The scar still reminds me of how Sheetal was always there. But before assuaging my sadness, she would try and divert my attention first.

'You missed the best lesson today,' she said that day, breaking the silence. 'Did you know that chickens make eggs?'

She snorted and laughed again, waiting for my reaction. 'Um, you hate eating eggs but love chicken!' She continued to laugh but it didn't work. She switched tracks.

'We'll be going home this weekend. You can speak to your parents then,' she said, swinging her legs.

Home. Sheetal had been visiting home every fortnight, gathering all the love and pampering that would see her through another fortnight, and always returned beaming. Besides, she had her siblings with her; boarding school was a home away from home for her. I was yearning for that fuzzy feeling, the kind you get from sipping on hot chocolate, wrapped up in a blanket.

'I want to go home too. To *my* home,' I said.

'Where is your home? Where have your parents moved to?' Sheetal asked.

Over many phone calls, Papa had told me that our family had moved because of a new job opportunity. He used to work in a factory, five minutes from our bungalow, as a mechanical engineer. I was happy in Kota, unaware that he was miserable because he struggled to make ends meet. This despair coincided with an irresistible opportunity in an industry that couldn't be more different than mechanical engineering: textiles. His courageous, unfathomable move changed four lives forever.

'Japan,' I replied. Neither of us had any idea where that was.

'Why didn't you go with them?' Sheetal asked.

My parents must have had a good reason, and they must have told me before enrolling me. They must have told me on the phone too, but I couldn't remember why. Or perhaps, I subconsciously chose not to because I was angry about being left behind. 'I don't know,' I said.

'When will you go to Japan?'

'Papa said in a few months.' I felt better as I said that out loud.

Until then, my plan was to count down to chicken curry once a week, a visit to Nani's house every fortnight, and an invitation to my unseen home in an unseen land soon. Home, although temporary, was Nani's house, where pampering was guaranteed and where I could at least speak to my parents.

5
A CRASH LANDING

March 1984, India

That weekend, my uncle, Savre Mama, arrived on his tatty, grey scooter to take me to Nani's house. An hour-long journey with no helmets, and limbs too short to either wrap around the scooter or Mama's potbelly, the ride was one hell of a mission. Although he was cuddly like a teddy bear, clinging to him still didn't stop me from praying for my life during the journey.

'Hold tight, *beta*,' Savre Mama said now and then. Apart from that, he didn't talk much. The traffic then was a free-for-all system. Keeping your wits about you was a matter of life and death. Every slant of the scooter, swerving around lorries and buses, reminded me to tighten my grip.

On the rare occasion that the family car was available, Savre Mama would pick me up in the parrot-green Ambassador, which resembled England's iconic black cabs. I searched longingly for its familiar number plate – CH7095 – as I waited by the steps outside the matron's office. I read the licence plates of every car that passed by even if it was obviously not a parrot-green Ambassador. Little habits like that can become innate behaviour that lasts into adulthood. I used to play a similar game with Kareena, asking her to read the number plates of cars on our daily walk to and from her Montessori school.

Nani's house was in a little alley off the high street in Karol Bagh, an area in Delhi famous for shopping. Traffic deadlocked with cars, motorbikes, lorries, bicycles, rickshaws, cows, dogs, and people rarely walking on the pavement was a typical scene. Electric wires from streetlights hung dangerously low, and lorries driving past would almost rip the wires loose. Almost. I would wince watching them each time. Billboards of the latest Bollywood movies stood tall at every crossroad, along with smaller posters on every streetlight. The pavements on either side of the road were filled with shoppers bargaining hard with shopkeepers. The fragrance of rich spices from scattered food stalls, and colourful shops selling everything from electronics to ornate saris, spoilt the senses. At Karol Bagh, chaos met charm.

The moment we pulled up outside the house, I skipped through the narrow, light blue hallway, calling out for Nani. I found her in the family room, as always. I ran into her arms and felt a familiar warmth, like Mummy's.

'What will you have, *meri gudia*? Shall I ask Chotu to get your favourite *halwa*? Or do you want *dosa* from our restaurant? *Besan laddoo* is your favourite, isn't it? Tell me, what will you have, my doll?' she asked.

Chotu was the family servant. Chotu, his nickname, meant 'the small one', and he was *chotu* in every sense – age, height, and stature. Only a few years older than me, he looked after the entire family.

'I'll have *dosa* and *besan laddoo*,' I said, looking at Chotu. He stopped all other chores for the day to obey my command. An instruction from a six-year-old to a twelve-year-old.

With my gaze locked on Nani, I watched her remind the laundry man, the milkman, and the driver of their duties for the day. Nani's gravitas drew everyone to her. Her soft features and circular face would have been comparable to a Bollywood actress if it weren't for smallpox scars that gave her a cobble-stoned appearance. She waddled around the house in her crisp, cotton sari, hair always braided. Tucked into her sari, tied tightly around her wholesome waistline, a clanking bunch of keys announced her presence. The keys were to a Godrej iron cupboard in her bedroom. To me, they were the portal to a magical world full of chocolates and sweets. The other items in her cupboard – saris, gold jewellery, some silver utensils, a few files, and lots of cash – were of no interest.

Nana, on the other hand, often seemed to be just another figure in the house. He was a man of few words and even fewer teeth. Yet there was a warmth to him like the winter sun. Sometimes he blended into the furniture as if he wasn't even there. Other times, everyone gathered around him in his room, making him the centre of attention.

The rest of the family numbered more than a cricket team. I had five uncles, three of them married with a couple of children each, and two aunts, one married. My uncles ran the family restaurant business on the main high street. The townhouse, three stories high and with steep staircases, was not for the faint-hearted. My thighs took a real beating going up and down several times daily. Iron grilles on every floor directly above the central courtyard helped avoid yet another journey; instructions, messages and plans for the day would be shouted up and down through the grille. Sometimes, a chain of communication was required when someone on the roof needed to convey a message to the ground floor.

'Chotu, get *dosa* from the restaurant for me.'

'Chotu, come upstairs.'

'I'll be down in ten minutes.'

'Children, come straight up and do your homework first.'

'Chotu, put the generator on. The electricity is out again.'

Throughout the day, voices dispersed from the grilles to every corner of the house. In the evening, the family would congregate in one room, packed like sardines. Most of my memories were formed in that modestly sized family room, just four metres squared. Add *crammed* to chaos and charm. There was so much love in that one room alone, there wasn't room for anything else, quite literally. And the noise level, with everyone talking over each other, was like standing in the middle of a live concert. We all used to play the 'who can speak the loudest to be heard' game.

This was my life when I was away from my parents. It made a refreshing change from the regimented life of boarding school. I ate what I wanted when I wanted, did what pleased me, and cuddled up with Nani before bedtime – until, of course, it was time for me to roll into my bed, wax cloth laid underneath the sheet. Nani had a plethora of bedtime stories, mostly of kings, queens, and their imperfect kingdoms, but none of them had me slumbering like my favourite bedtime story, *The Lion and the Hare*.

This evening was like every other at Nani's house. The

family room began to fill with people as the streetlights went on and the birds flew back to their nests. Food arrived in instalments too. Multiple conversations were going on, everyone dipping in and out of them. The soft-spoken ones listened, and the loud ones competed with one another. Within minutes, all conversations blended into one song-like hum of white noise. The noise, the food, the chaos, I sat there soaking it all in, hoping the joy would carry me through another two weeks at the boarding school. Among all this noise, I heard the first phone ring, shrill and startling, in Nana's room.

'That call is for you, Shweta,' said Savre Mama.

'How do you know?' I asked, hopeful.

'I just do,' he smiled. I clambered over the table, down again, weaved in and out of all the legs, and ran to pick up the black telephone receiver. Sitting on a brown, shabby couch next to the phone, my legs dangling, I was disappointed to hear a strange lady's sharp and squeaky voice on the other end, until she said, 'Call for Shweta from Japan.' I told her, the operator, that's me.

'Hello, *beta*!' yelled Papa a moment later. There was a constant crackling disturbance in the background. 'How are you settling in?'

'Papa!' I shouted back. 'Why can't I stay here with Nani and Kallo Mausi? I like it here.'

'Mausi is so young herself, still attending college. She won't be able to look after you. And, *beta*, a visit to the grandparents' home is always more fun if it's short and sweet.'

This sounded like an excuse to me. I responded with louder, longer breaths. He replied by changing the subject.

'Tell me about your friends.'

'Um, where's Mummy?' I asked, following suit. Papa passed the phone to her.

'Hello, *beta*,' Mummy's voice was softer, soothing. 'Are you eating well in the boarding school? And don't forget the wax cloth under the sheet every day.'

'Mummy?' I fidgeted with the circular white dial, sticking my fingers in each hole, working my way through the numbers.

'Yes?'

I hesitated. I wanted to moan to her about having to wash my sheets every day. A good, hearty moan. After all, I should not have been expected to do that. That was the cleaning ladies' job.

'Yes, *beta*? What is it?'

How could I, though? If I did, I would be complaining to someone who had washed my sheets for years, and I would be interrupting her well-deserved break. How could I worry her about it all over again?

'We're on an international call, *beta*. It's very expensive.'

'Mummy. . .Mummy, I have to wash my sheet by myself,' I said, feeling instant relief. A pressure cooker releasing a whistle. I dared not speak of this in front of the matron. Although the frequency of communication with my parents had reduced, at least I was able to share without reservations.

'What?! Don't the cleaning ladies do it?'

'No.'

'Papa and I will speak to the matron tomorrow.'

'When will I see you? I want to be with you.'

'Very soon. Nani will receive your aeroplane ticket soon.'

I can't remember if the phone line got disconnected or if the conversation ended there. We weren't a family who expressed love with effusive goodbyes. Yet the short call was an injection of love and the hope of unity.

Back in the other room, I buried my head in Nani's lap and wailed. I could feel everyone's pitying eyes on me. There was a brief moment of silence before the conversations resumed. Then my aunt, Sona Mami, entered. She liked encouraging me to dance at any opportunity. Sometimes, like that evening, it was to fill an awkward moment. When it came to dancing, even tears wouldn't stop me.

'Shweta, we haven't seen you perform for us in a while,' she said.

Everyone stopped as though a choir conductor had signalled the end of the song. I clambered onto the coffee table even as people were clearing their food plates. There was no stopping me, singing and dancing to *She'll Be Comin' Round the Mountain*. That coffee table was my mountain, and I was determined to dance my way to the peak. Never mind sports, I had all the stamina I needed for dance. I usually wouldn't stop until someone asked me to. A few minutes must have passed. My cheeks were hot, my breath short and quick. This only spurred me on. The more breathless I became, the more elated I felt, endorphins dancing through my veins. With everyone cheering me on, I felt delirious . . . until another aunt, Maya Mami, interrupted.

'You've turned from black to purple, like an aubergine, from all the dancing,' she said, tugging my left arm. 'Come down now.'

I hadn't the faintest idea what she meant. I didn't particularly care for Maya Mami, so I carried on dancing. Maya Mami's delicate features disguised her sharp tongue. She looked after me well, like the others did, but her capricious temper and uncouth ways often cancelled out the care she gave.

'She enjoys it and is very talented. Let her dance,' Sona Mami said, surprised by the intrusion.

'What is she going to gain from all this dancing? It's not like she can become a Bollywood actress.'

A Bollywood actress is *exactly* what I wanted to become. I stopped dancing, tuning in to the quarrel.

'Why can't she?'

'Have you not seen her colour? There's no room for *kali* actresses in Bollywood.'

'Well, she can make room for herself.'

'Don't give her false hopes.'

Sona Mami left the room, leaving me filled with questions. Everyone continued chattering, their white noise mixing with the questions in my head – a confusing cocktail. I wished Papa had called now. I wished I could ask him about colour, about why colour mattered, if colour *should* matter – like I used to bombard him with questions on our walks to the local shops, sitting on his shoulders.

'*Bas*, no more, Shweta,' he used to say. 'Save some for tomorrow.'

The family in the room didn't seem one bit concerned by what had happened; they were oblivious to my confusion. I headed to Sona Mami's room.

This was my first crash course in the fairness barometer, the Fairometer. But more than the crash course itself, what infuriated me was the forced crash landing while I was blissfully enjoying twirling around. Being denied little pleasures as a child.

Standing in Sona Mami's doorway, I realised I wasn't upset about the interruption after all. The subject of the conversation hit me, like referred and delayed pain; it was the conclusion of the argument that sank my heart. I asked her, 'Can't I become an actress because of my dark colour? Why do only fair women make it to Bollywood?'

'Of course, you can, *beta*. There are people in this world who believe that fair skin is beautiful. But look at you, you are beautiful. And talented. I am sure you'll be what you want to be.'

Her comforting words were exactly what a pathetically optimistic little girl needed to hear. That talent was all that mattered. That no career was out of reach because of skin tone. That we lived in a fair, egalitarian world. Nonetheless, I couldn't dismiss this distasteful introduction to my colour. Until then, whenever I looked in a mirror, I only saw a six-year-old girl.

Shweta Khandelwal, daughter of Satish and Veena Khandelwal, suffers from bedwetting (but that will fix itself), and is passionate about dance.

I inched towards Sona Mami's dressing table mirror and examined myself. Having just learned that colour, when it came to certain careers, was a defining identity, was *kali* to be mine, above everything else?

I examined my aunt, milky white with the slightest hint

of caramel, a natural beauty that would light up rooms; beauty that makeup would tarnish rather than enhance as though God had taken a day off to sculpt her. As far as Indian complexion goes, there was no doubt Sona Mami was *gori-chitti*. She was free from colour prejudice; her husband, my uncle, was *kala*. His nickname was Kale. The fact that your colour could become your name haunted me. One by one, my head filled with all those family members whose names were based on their colour. Then, when my mind wandered away from family names and towards Bollywood, I realised that most villains in the movies were named 'Kalia', derived from 'black'. And sure enough, their skin tone was very dark. Colour-based nicknames weren't just our family thing. Bollywood used them too.

The nickname that broke my heart was Kallo, the name given to my mother's sister. Although a college student, she cared for me like her own child. Petite and demure, she rarely contributed to any family conversations, but her incredible smile spoke a thousand words. She was as soft as cotton candy in every way. I only ever saw her in two neat plaits, ribbons tied in perfect bows at the tail-end and not a trace of make-up. We had a strong resemblance, so much so that on many occasions outsiders would ask if she was my mother. We were the same colour, yet I had never stopped to think why her nickname was Kallo. I felt overwhelmed with guilt because I was among those who addressed her with that name – I had done so earlier during the call with Papa. In fact, I didn't know her real name.

'What's Kallo Mausi's real name?' I asked Sona Mami.

'Sangeeta.'

Sangeeta. Music. Resembling her speech, silky and heart-warming.

'Why does everyone call her by that horrible name, Kallo, then? Why does she not say something?'

'I don't know. I guess it doesn't bother her.'

It bothered me. If she was Kallo, was I going to be called Kallo Junior? That day surely wasn't far off, given that others in the family had such nicknames. It wasn't just for the fear of my name changing. I couldn't allow myself to be a party to the name-calling. From that day, Kallo Mausi became Sangeeta Mausi. For the rest of the day, I addressed her as Sangeeta Mausi, my volume raised a notch, ensuring everyone heard, loud and clear. The name signified who she was, rather than her colour. She noticed the change in how I addressed her but didn't acknowledge it with words. She didn't have to because her delicious smile did. I established a new, deeper bond with her, like those in a herd sticking together.

I thought I could change the world – well, at least the family – call everyone by their real names and soon enough everyone would start doing the same. Real people with real identities. Simple. The naive attempt of a righteous six-year-old to bring about change in adults unwilling to change. The colour prejudice was so deeply entrenched, they didn't recognise the need for change. And sure enough, I was given a taste of this the next morning, before Savre Mama and I departed for the boarding school.

Sangeeta Mausi was about to leave for college. Standing in the narrow hallway leading to the entrance of the house, I was in no rush to say goodbye, sharing all sorts of stories from boarding school. Each one of my sentences had a permanent prefix – Sangeeta Mausi. Maya Mami was rushing back and forth, getting her son ready for school. Once again, she interrupted.

'By calling her Sangeeta, her colour won't change. She's still *kali* and so are you.'

This time I turned purple from rage, but Sangeeta Mausi remained nonchalant. She said goodbye to me and disappeared. Her indifference annoyed me.

During the hour-long journey back to boarding school, I sat hushed on the scooter, preoccupied with what I had experienced the entire weekend.

'You're awfully quiet today,' observed Savre Mama.

'Mama, why is everyone in the family so mean to Sangeeta Mausi? Why do they call her Kallo? And why doesn't she stop them?'

'Oh, *beta*, it's all in jest. It doesn't mean anything.'

'That's easy for you to say. She's the one who's called a name by her colour.'

'I am too.'

'What do you mean?'

'My name, Savre, is also a shade of skin tone, not as dark as *kala*. Lighter than that. But I don't mind. I know it's out of love.'

'I think that's mean.'

'You won't understand. Don't take it too seriously.'

He was right. I couldn't comprehend how giving someone a nickname based on their colour was an expression of love. But what I understood was that the Fairometer had more skin-tone terms than I had realised, including *saavre* derived from *saanvla* or *saanvli* – bronze. Three out of four modules were completed on the crash course over one weekend visit to my second home.

Back at boarding school, at least one burden had been lifted off my shoulders: no more washing of heavy, drenched sheets. Mummy would have called the matron by now, complaining about the situation. The cleaning ladies would take care of my sheets from now on.

The next morning, I left the sheet in the bathroom and found it exactly as it was later that afternoon, smelling even worse. I didn't have the slightest doubt that Mummy hadn't called. I blamed the notoriously lazy cleaning ladies. Like everything else, I started to get used to the encumbrance of washing the sheets myself and didn't mention it again during phone calls. Or perhaps I forgot to. I can't exactly remember.

I carried the burden of the Fairometer crash course in my gut, though. I continued visiting Nani's every fortnight. No further harsh colour conversations were had. Still, digesting that one lesson felt like trying to digest putrid food. I needed to flush it out of my system, but I didn't know how. It lingered, attaching itself to the justification 'It's all in jest.' I tried to see the funny side in colour-induced name-calling but there was nothing humorous about it. When I confided in Sheetal, she brushed it off saying, 'It's not a big deal. It's only a nickname.'

Maybe it wasn't a big deal after all. Anything Sheetal said was like God's word. She had a way with me, pacifying me. In her presence, I could shake off the lesson. But Nani's house was the exact opposite. Despite all the love, warmth, and comfort I received, the house encouraged colour-based nicknames such as Kale, Kallo, and Savre. For all of the family's virtues, this was their one vice. But because no one objected, I silenced myself. With my lips sealed, witnessing the name-calling was as tortuous as my silence in the face of Payal's taunts. I loathed myself for my complicity. At bedtime, I promised myself that I would speak up, but would wake up feeling cowardly.

I realised what I was afraid of in both instances – facing possible adverse reactions without my two pillars of strength, my parents, by my side. Each day began to drag because of my silence. Spotting aeroplanes in the sky daily brought a burst of excitement. A reminder of the day I could bask in the shade of my pillars.

6

AN ANSWERED PRAYER

June 1984, Japan

A charming air hostess greeted me at the door of the Air India aircraft, then took my hand and led me down the aisle. She resembled a plump, middle-aged Indian Barbie doll, in a printed, maroon sari. Her hair was tucked in a bun, not a single strand out of place, and she wore the brightest red lipstick. I followed her, wide-eyed, gazing at the pristine seats and the lights on the panel above them. The white tube-like casing of the plane was unlike anything I had seen. The trains I used to take between Kota and Delhi were very different, with their cold, hard metal berths that forced you to sit upright. The plane seats looked inviting.

The air hostess gathered it was my first time. She settled me into my seat, ruffled my hair, and clasped the seatbelt. 'We'll be landing in Osaka in ten hours. I will be sitting here, opposite you, if you need anything,' she smiled.

Ten whole hours to myself. All the planes had in those days was one screen at the front of either aisle which played one old Bollywood movie for the entire cabin. But the music collection was so dreary that I resorted to watching the movie. Every time the air hostess returned to her seat for a break, I insisted on playing Snap with a deck of cards. I also bored her with endless questions about the mechanics of the plane.

'Come with me. I can show you the pilot's cockpit,' she whispered, looking around to confirm that the rest of the passengers were fast asleep. I didn't know what to expect but understood that this was a big moment. I danced my way up the stairs of the jumbo jet, the end of which led to the cockpit's door, ajar. Of the two pilots, one looked stern, the other, friendly. The friendly one talked me through a few buttons and how things worked. Nothing sank in. The lit-up buttons on the control panel resembled one of Delhi's rush-hour traffic jams – a sea of bright yellow and red taillights. But the view from the cockpit's windshield was endless darkness, like a black hole. What I remember most was how the handsome pilots, dressed in brilliant white uniforms, controlled the enormous plane with ease. It looked a lot simpler than riding a scooter in ground traffic.

Three more hours until we landed. I grew even more anxious to see my parents, to share this once-in-a-lifetime opportunity given to me. I asked the air hostess if we could go back to the cockpit and ask the pilots to drive faster.

'Planes don't work like that,' she laughed, turning my light off and wrapping me up in a blanket. She wanted me to sleep and had lost the will to answer any more questions.

At Itami International Airport in Osaka, the air hostess told me to look out for my family when the Green Channel's doors opened. Although this was my first time in Japan, I don't remember noticing anything about the country.

My eyes were searching for one and only one person.

'Papa!' I ran towards him. He looked exactly how I remembered him, always immaculately dressed. A blue check shirt tucked into his grey bell-bottom trousers, held by a black belt high around his waist. Black hair combed neatly, a couple of waves in the front disrupting the effort, gave him a softer look. So did his double chin. A black Titan watch, strapped on his milky white wrist, gleamed from a distance. Papa's colour scored 1 on the Fairometer: *gora-chitta*.

Seeing me, Papa too, hurried closer. I was inches away from wrapping myself around his leg when the air hostess held me back. 'I'm sorry, sir! She must be mistaken. She's looking for her father,' she said.

'I *am* her father,' said Papa, sweeping me into his arms.

'Oh!' she replied, flustered. 'I'm terribly sorry, sir.'

I hugged Papa so hard that my chest hurt. My lungs inhaled joy and exhaled all memories of the boarding school and Karol Bagh. Payal, washing bed sheets, the Fairometer, everything prior to the plane ride vanished. Papa asked me how I was.

'I saw the cockpit! I saw the cockpit!' I sang.

The air hostess, a spare part in our reunion, waved goodbye.

'Where's Mummy?' My eyes scanned the crowd but couldn't find her.

'She's at home with Neeraj. She couldn't leave him alone.'

I sighed. Neeraj was my eighteen-month-old brother whom I didn't remember much. I don't even remember asking for him and how he was during any of our phone conversations.

Two buses and a short uphill walk later, we stood outside the front door of our third-floor apartment in Kobe. Mummy greeted me with a whimpering Neeraj perched on her hip, his skinny legs wrapped around her waist. I took solace in her tears of joy, knowing that she had missed me too. Mummy passed my brother on to Papa and embraced me. How I had missed those arms. I had pictured this moment a million times in my daydreams; my imagination couldn't compare to the delight of reality.

But Neeraj didn't let that moment last too long. He started wailing in Papa's arms, leaning his body towards Mummy. He got his way, and Mummy extricated herself from me and pulled him into her arms. As ecstatic as I was to be home, beneath the happiness brewed an unfamiliar emotion towards an unfamiliar sibling: jealousy.

Neeraj didn't just get his way on this occasion. He seemed accustomed to getting his way. In fact, he had defied all odds and was in control of his own birth. During his delivery in December 1982, Neeraj passed faeces into the amniotic fluid. Due to severe complications, the doctor said he could only save one life, either Mummy's or Neeraj's. Papa chose Mummy. Miraculously, the doctor saved both, although Neeraj had us all hanging. He was born unconscious; the doctor had to rub and gently slap his back several times, encouraging him to breathe. A few moments later, my brother made his grandiose entrance into the world.

Since then, he became suffocatingly precious to my parents, and life for the family spiralled in a direction none of us had envisaged in our wildest dreams. The aunts in Karol Bagh used to say, 'Neeraj has brought *achchi kismat*, good fate, for the family.' But his fate's plan didn't include me. Fourteen months after my brother's arrival, my parents moved with Neeraj into the new home in Kobe. Four months later, when I arrived, I felt like a visitor in *his* home.

Over the next few weeks, I shadowed Mummy like a smitten pet, trying to make this unfamiliar house my home too. Even going to the shops excited me, despite having to help her carry bags of shopping, panting as we walked back uphill. When we reached the apartment, getting a pushchair and shopping bags up the stairs was a physical and mental challenge. Mummy would manoeuvre Neeraj's pushchair up first, asking me to wait by all the bags. Then she would leave the pushchair by the front door but bring Neeraj back down, straddled around her waist. Finally, we would both carry as many bags up as we could, Neeraj whining the entire time. Mummy was an adroit homemaker. Her positive attitude towards finding solutions to everyday problems was both underestimated and under-appreciated. Like the time when our VCR stopped playing movies clearly. She had read in some Hindi magazine that the VCR head was most likely in need of a clean and that nail varnish remover did the trick. She unscrewed the device, figured out where the head was, dabbed some remover on a Q-Tip and cleaned it assiduously. The VCR played movies again like it was brand new. She used to say, 'There's always a *jugaad*, a quick fix, to everything.' She could have run classes to teach the art of *jugaad*.

Every day in Kobe was a dream: delectable home-cooked meals, my favourite Japanese snack, Tongari Corn, stacked in the kitchen cupboard, watching Doraemon cartoons whenever the TV channels played them, and sometimes visiting my parents' friends for dinner. Sundays were my favourite, splashing in the bath with Papa and Neeraj in a bathroom that was oversized for a one-bedroom apartment. Custard-yellow tiles from floor to ceiling and light blue mats and bath curtains – neither of the two colours appealed to me but bath time did. Mummy wasn't too happy about me joining in. Every Sunday, she would say, 'You're a big girl now, Shweta. You shouldn't be in there with Neeraj and Papa.'

I would stand crying by the bathtub in my underpants, knowing that I could melt Papa's heart in moments. He would then say, 'Let her join us, she's still a child.' Once, only once, did he come out with the words, 'It's not like she'll be here for long.'

'Where will I be, Papa?' I questioned.

Papa fell silent.

'You said I'll only be in the boarding school for a few months!'

Never mind how I felt about a crushed hope, I will never forget the look on his face, dripping with guilt. The look of having let someone down. He did what he was good at - changing the subject by cracking a joke. He had a way with humour. The way he narrated jokes with such passion, giggling as he did, had his audience laughing out loud, even at the worst ones.

As I wasn't going to be in Kobe for long, exploring the city was not on my agenda because it meant diverting Mummy and Papa's attention away from me. But we did step out sometimes. And everywhere we went – which wasn't far without a car – Kobe reminded me of Kota, although if the

Oxford Dictionary were to define the opposite of Kota, Kobe would be the likely entry. Sometimes, though, opposites are so far apart that they come around a full circle. Having focused so hard on the differences, I noticed one similarity. The reason why Kobe reminded me so much of Kota was because both Kota and Kobe represented our happy family of *four*.

There was a similarity between Kobe and Virendra Gram Boarding School too: the lush mountains. They were my black gates. I had yet to see what existed on the other side, but I wasn't one bit curious, not yet. Confinement in the prison within the black gates was suffocating, and I repeatedly sought paradise outside. The natural enclosure created by the mountain range cast a warm, protective shadow over the city. It *was* my paradise. Liberating, comforting, and flawless. Roads so clean you could eat off them. The traffic system, impeccable. Compact Japanese houses and buildings, mirroring compact Japanese people. Immaculate trains with gleaming carriages. Courteous and soft-spoken citizens.

None of this impressed me as much as a Baskin-Robbins ice cream parlour, minutes away from our apartment on the way to the local grocery store, Co-op. The lady in the ice cream parlour wore layers of pale foundation to conceal the wrinkles around her eyes and her upper lip. A good attempt. She had taken a particular liking to Mummy.

'*Mei oki ne, mei kirei ne, Veena san.* Your eyes are big, your eyes are beautiful,' she would say. Mummy would blush, then giggle, then respond with, '*Arigato*, thank you.'

'*Neeraji kun kawai ne.* Little Neeraj is very cute,' she would also say. She never said anything about me.

One sunlit afternoon, as per usual, we stopped at Baskin Robbins on our way to Co-op. The parlour lady had completed her drill of complimenting Mummy and Neeraj. We stood by the pedestrian crossing, me slurping my chocolate chip ice cream, Neeraj fussing in the stroller. Mummy, in her favourite navy-blue sari, was pacifying him when I spotted several children walking up to the crossing. Girls in blue-and-white-striped uniform dresses, a yellow badge on their left collar. Boys in white shirts and grey shorts. Mothers holding their school bags. *There's a school here?*

'Why can't I go to this school, Mummy?' I asked, recalling Papa's words, 'She won't be here for long.'

'Hmmm?' Mummy said, fixing Neeraj's blue sipper.

'Why can't I go to this school and live here?' I pointed at the children flooding to the crossing, chattering in English.

'Uh, very soon, *beta*.' Mummy's face dropped. 'Come on, the light's turned green.'

'Why can Neeraj be with you and not me?'

'Because Neeraj is a toddler. He doesn't need to go to school.'

'I know why Neeraj is with you,' I said, finishing the last bite of my cone. 'He's brought good *kismat* for the family. That's why.'

'Where did you hear that?!' Mummy asked, perturbed.

'All the aunties in India say it.'

'Never, ever believe that. We want the best for you. Your education cannot be interrupted, and we cannot afford this school here, not yet. That's all.'

'Why can't I go to any other school then?'

'There are only two English-speaking schools in Kobe, *beta*. Both are private schools with very high fees. And Japanese schools only take Japanese children.'

I sulked, realising there were no other options.

'You will be here soon. In that school,' Mummy said, grabbing the shopping basket at Co-op. 'Now, you push the stroller and I'll shop.'

It broke my heart that my parents couldn't afford my education in Japan. It broke theirs too. They disguised it well, though. If only Neeraj's lucky charm could land Papa a job with a bigger pay cheque. But he reserved his lucky charm for himself. He did not need formal schooling, only infinite attention. So, Neeraj got his way simply by being a helpless infant.

I glared at my little brother, curled up in the stroller fast asleep. And I prayed for him to disappear – only for a few days so that I could enjoy some undivided attention. It wasn't much to ask for, was it, knowing that he would get the same for ten months when I returned to India?

'Can you look after Neeraj?' said Mummy. 'He's asleep in the bedroom. I need to pop to the shop for groceries. I'll be back before he wakes up.'

Two weeks before the summer holiday ended it was her turn to host a dinner party for her friends. With only a few hours to prepare, pushing Neeraj's buggy uphill overloaded with shopping bags, was only going to slow her down.

I peered into the room and nodded. Neeraj was in a deep sleep in the mid-afternoon summer heat that kept the apartment toasty. Mummy's open wardrobe was tempting me to play dress-up. As she reached for the main door, I reached for one of her saris.

I wanted to emulate Mummy's look. Her fair skin was as flawless as a fresh blanket of snow. Big, black eyes complemented her complexion. She carried her sari with grace, and always wore a maroon *bindi* matched with her lipstick. Effortless, unassuming beauty.

With a sari wrapped around my dress belt, I stumbled to the bathroom. I looked like a participant in a sack race, clutching the sari with both hands so it didn't undrape itself. Still, the finishing touches were important. I reached up for a *bindi* in the bathroom cabinet and smeared on some lipstick. I still didn't look like her. Something was missing. In the cabinet, on the top shelf, was Neeraj's talcum powder. I clambered onto the toilet seat, stretched my arm, grabbed the powder, and dabbed it all over my face. Now I looked like her: fairer. When I look back on this incident, I wonder if this little dress-up act was where my hypocrisy was born. Or 'confusion' might be a better word at that age. I had already forgotten how my heart had sunk when Maya Mami called me *kali*. All I wanted was to look like my mother.

Back in the bedroom, I admired myself in the wardrobe's mirror. Pretty, like Mummy.

Just then, I heard keys jangling in the main door. Mummy was back. She trudged into the bedroom, several shopping bags in both hands weighing her down. My attire didn't provoke any reaction, but she looked distressed.

'Why was the front door wide open?' She turned to the bed. 'Where is Neeraj?'

'He was here, sleeping the whole time.'

'He's not here, Shweta!'

We both called for him, searching under the bed and in the wardrobe. Mummy rushed to the bathroom in case he was trying to use the potty. Not there. She searched every nook and cranny. I couldn't bring myself to help her. I stood rooted to the spot with fear and guilt. A million thoughts swirled in my head as I searched for possible outcomes to the situation. None of them ended well for me.

Mummy was hysterical. 'How can you not know where he is? And be so irresponsible? I asked you to look after him, not dress up!'

'I, I don't know. Maybe you didn't lock the door…'

'I locked it before I left!'

Mummy continued to search for him everywhere, going around in circles. She went up to the roof terrace, down the road, and to all neighbouring areas, as far as an eighteen-month-old child could have toddled off on his own.

When she left the apartment, I stepped out of the bedroom, undraped the sari, and dusted off the powder. I searched for Neeraj in my favourite hiding spots that Mummy had missed, places where I would conceal myself when we played hide and seek together. Behind the bathroom curtain, inside the shoe cupboard, under the coffee table, and behind the TV unit – but there was no sign of him anywhere!

I couldn't make any sense of what was happening and stayed clear of Mummy's field of vision and her wrath. Curled up in one corner of the living room, I watched her fall on the couch in despair and call Papa at last.

'Neeraj is not in the house! I can't find him anywhere. I went shopping when he was sleeping and came back to find he'd gone! The front door was open,' she cried. Her words travelled at the speed of light. I inferred that Papa hadn't caught any of that because she repeated everything, slower this time.

Papa rushed through the door an hour later, a lit cigarette in his hand, his companion during the stressful train journey. He had informed the police before he left his office. Two policemen arrived minutes later, running through the entire incident as though it was a crime scene. After they made notes, Papa called some close friends. He fiddled with the telephone cord, leaving it tangled. But his voice was poised and showed no signs of panic.

Every phone call ended with, 'If you do see him, call me immediately, won't you? Thank you.' We were expecting some of these friends over for dinner in a few hours. Sure enough, that was cancelled.

Papa and Mummy were locked in a heated argument. I couldn't bear watching them argue. I wanted to run out that open door myself, run to the mountains all the way to the other side. Perhaps the other side had identical families, happy, cloned families where no one argued. The Japanese police officers received their first dose of Indian family drama – a cacophony of melodramatic voices and sobbing. Papa criticised Mummy for leaving me, a six-year-old, in charge of a toddler. Mummy justified that she had been carrying shopping bags and Neeraj's pushchair uphill for months. She needed a break.

'I only had a few hours to make dinner before everyone arrives.'

'To hell with the dinner! Look at our girl. She's petrified.'

He managed to cajole me out of the corner and onto his lap, trying to ensure I didn't hold myself responsible. But I did because I *had* prayed for Neeraj's disappearance!

Little did I know that of all the prayers, the Almighty would accept this one, under such circumstances. Neeraj couldn't have timed it better. Disappearing in a shopping mall or in a park would have worked well. But from our home, under my watch – if he was not found, I would never be forgiven. I wasn't concerned about my lost little brother. I was more worried about my diminishing chances of staying in Kobe. I worried that the boarding school would be my main residence forever.

Then the phone rang.

'*Hai. Hai*,' Papa said that a lot, nodding on the phone.

'*Daijoubu desu ka*? Is he all right?' This was a phrase I had picked up from numerous visits to the local park. Mothers would often say this when their children fell or injured themselves. Neeraj must have been *daijoubu*; colour returned to Papa's pale face.

'*Domo arigato gozaimashita.*' I caught the last sentence that Papa spoke and the very first sentence that he had taught me. *Thank you very much.*

Over an hour after his disappearance, the police found Neeraj on the main road halfway between our apartment and Sannomiya train station. This baffled all three of us. We contemplated the possible series of events. Nothing made sense because nothing sensational or disturbing was ever featured in the news in Japan. I'd not heard of any murders, burglaries, or protests. Once, when we planned on visiting Papa's office in Osaka, the train station apologised three times for a train delayed by fifteen seconds. That train delay made it to the news! That was pretty much as exciting as local news got in Japan.

How could an eighteen-month-old have left a locked

apartment on his own? An adult must have been responsible.

I insisted on going with Papa to the *koban*, the police station, situated opposite Sannomiya station. After all their investigations, checking for any signs of physical harm or trauma, the police concluded that Neeraj was most likely sleepwalking. They found him walking in a daze, oblivious to his surroundings. He fell into a deep sleep as soon as an officer picked him up.

When we entered the police station, we found Neeraj sitting on the bench by one of the officer's desks, sipping on orange juice from a carton. As I scurried in with Papa, gripping his right hand's little finger, I stared at Neeraj. He wasn't wearing any pants!

'Papa *hoshi*. Papa *hoshi*,' babbled Neeraj, seeing us. 'Want Papa. Want Papa.' He spoke better Japanese than Hindi or English.

Papa looked perplexed. Then, as usual, he saw the situation's funny side. 'The least you could have done was put some pants on before stepping out.'

I had a barrage of questions for Papa on our way home. The conclusion that Neeraj was sleepwalking was worse than kidnapping or something of that sort. How could a toddler open a door, pitter-patter down two sets of staircases with his skinny bowlegs – legs that had only recently learned to walk – and navigate his way through crossroads? All in his sleep? Papa said sleepwalking is a rare condition, a mystery to medical science in many ways. He said sleepwalkers can have elevated senses to get about, and they cannot recollect their experiences because they are semi-conscious. This sounded spookily similar to a ghost story that Payal had once forced us to listen to at boarding school. It was the only time I didn't wet my bed because I didn't sleep all night!

Elevated senses. Semi-conscious.

I knew it! Neeraj wasn't even supposed to be here. He always got his way with his lucky charm; he must have supernatural powers.

I convinced myself that this was the only answer to the inexplicable incident; that his angelic persona was in fact devilish. But I also rode a rollercoaster of other emotions: guilt about praying for his disappearance, sympathy for all that his little body must have experienced during sleepwalking, and envy. A precious bundle to my parents, this incident was only going to land him in a sea of empathy, waves of attention swirling around him.

Rest assured, I didn't pray again for a while, not even to leave boarding school for good. I didn't have faith in prayers. What if the Almighty accepted the opposite? I felt sorry for my parents, though. As if my bedwetting wasn't enough, they now had two children with two different conditions, both triggered in deep sleep. One sleepwalking child and one bedwetter. The only difference was that a sleepwalking toddler invited sympathy; a bedwetting six-year-old brought disdain.

It'll fix itself. Those were the only words I had faith in. I had a fortnight to fix my problem before returning to Virendra Gram. And if I did, I could get my share of attention. Wholeheartedly. Maybe even take back from Neeraj the share of parental love that had been showered on him in my absence. Better yet, I could take *all* his share of the love because if my bedwetting ended, and he was still sleepwalking, I would be the better child, the favourite one.

7

BULLSEYE!

The Same Evening

Kisses, lots of kisses. Mummy planted copious amounts of affection on Neeraj's cheeks at the apartment doorstep. For a moment I wished I had gone missing. I wished I had received that many kisses when I first arrived home.

Papa had called her from the police station, filling her in on the police officer's conclusions. She dismissed it in disbelief and said they should save the detailed discussion for later. Some friends were coming over anyway and were bringing food. It was a very kind gesture, but after the stress we had all been through, having people over was the last thing we needed.

At 7 p.m. sharp, adopting Japanese punctuality, the friends started arriving to meet the star of the day, Neeraj. Every single one of them pinched his cheeks, kissed him. His sleepwalking incident lent itself to becoming an amusing story for a dinner table conversation.

Neeraj and I had eaten before the adults sat down.

Overcompensating for my guilt, I kept him entertained with toys, one ear tuned into the adults' conversation.

'Have you ever found him sleepwalking before today?' asked Mrs Sharma.

'Where did the police find him?' enquired Mrs Singh.

'Does anyone else in your family sleepwalk?' asked Mrs Gujral. 'You should see a doctor about it. You know, Mrs Kapadia, had a daughter who unfortunately passed away from such an incident. She was thirteen and used to sleepwalk. She fell off their apartment balcony many years ago.'

Mrs Gujral, known for impeccable timing in giving unsolicited advice, reminded me of Maya Mami, both because of their similar appearance and their ways. Mummy and Papa hadn't had time to digest the entire incident yet. They had received the police officer's conclusion with some scepticism. Discussing it with others was not on the agenda, let alone learning about any possible dramatic consequences.

Silence filled the room, aside from the clanking cutlery. All eyes including mine were locked on Neeraj. Up until then, I saw him as an angelically devilish child, one who was up to mischief, one who was born with mysterious sleepwalking superpowers. Now I saw him as an innocent toddler, roaming the streets of Kobe, oblivious to the fact that he could be the biggest danger to himself. I picked him up, sat him on my lap, and planted lots of kisses on his face. All my feelings of envy evaporated at that moment. Sisterly love bubbled to the surface. To think that I could have lost my little brother filled me with a desire to protect him.

'Mrs. Gujral, thank you for your concern,' Papa said, breaking the silence. 'We'll get Neeraj seen by a doctor.

Shall we carry on with dinner? We've had a stressful day.' His firm suggestion should have put a stop to any further prying. But Mrs Gujral's eyes were still locked on Neeraj. When they shifted to me, I realised she was examining me too.

'Look at him, adorable and innocent,' she said. 'How is your son so fair and your daughter this dark? They don't look like siblings.' She laughed as if to trivialise the effect of the bomb she just dropped.

Bullseye. That hit home.

This was the first time I took real notice of Neeraj's appearance. Or perhaps I had noticed him already but the difference in our looks hadn't registered. Curly locks down to his shoulders, small eyes with long lashes, a cute butterball as a toddler should be, and skin tone a beautiful blend of peach and gold. Aside from crying all the time, he was annoyingly adorable, born with great fate, *and* with my parents' complexion.

I was all ears, awaiting my parents' responses. The question – *Why was I different?* – had not fully formed in my mind. Now that someone else had vocalised it, the intensity of the question expanded like a balloon about to burst.

Mummy broke the silence this time. 'I was still young and naive when she was born, only twenty. When she was a baby, I made the mistake of massaging her daily with mustard oil and then leaving her to bask in the sun. She wasn't born dark.'

I wasn't? This news brought hope, comforted me. If I wasn't born dark, then it could be fixed. Somewhere beneath the first layer of my dark skin, lay fair skin. All I had to do was figure out a way of revealing that layer.

But I didn't know how. I didn't have a plan. I was just glad that it was fixable. I transferred all my energy from fixing my bedwetting to fixing my skin instead. On the surface, I understood the reason for having to return to boarding school: education. When my parents emphasised its importance, I would nod along like an obedient, studious child. But deep in my mind, I didn't care about learning. What I cared more about was looking like my parents. Denial led to desperate attempts. Anything to stay at home.

At boarding school, I used to lie on a soggy sheet, daydreaming of escaping through the black gates. Now, I lay daydreaming of fair skin. I knew that this wouldn't fix itself. It required intervention. A *jugaad*. If I applied the talcum powder every day, it would blend with my dark skin tone to reveal a lighter shade. I had learned this in art class: add white to any colour to create a lighter shade. This was foolproof; I had seen it with my own eyes. This was my *jugaad*. I tried this remedy daily.

While this routine preoccupied me, Neeraj went missing from the apartment again the following Saturday. Thank goodness I couldn't be blamed this time. Papa searched for him on our road, Mummy walked down Tor Road, towards Baskin-Robbins, and I stood outside the building to keep an eye out for him. Papa eventually found my brother outside the Lawson convenience store on our road, five minutes from the apartment. As soon as Papa picked him up, Neeraj fell asleep. After that day, the landlord installed a chain on the front door and a gate on the stairs leading up to the roof terrace. Protecting Neeraj became my parents' top priority while protecting myself became mine. I kept applying the talcum powder, convinced that it would make a difference. It turned out to be fruitless. My colour didn't fix itself and I had no more stops to pull out.

Two weeks passed, and I was back at Itami International Airport, bawling my eyes out by the check-in counter, praying to see the same air hostess again. There was no point in praying for anything else.

8

FLAMES

July 1984, India

I left my family behind on the foothills of the mountains in Kobe, wistfully waving goodbye from the aeroplane. During the ten-hour flight, I told myself that embracing Virendra Gram for the next ten months was my only choice.

I felt more at ease when I passed through its black gates in July 1984. Familiarity made a great comfort blanket. In my suitcase were a few extra items: a pink Hello Kitty nightie, a couple of boxes of my favourite Japanese snack, Tongari Corn, a surplus of holiday memories, and one nagging question: did I really have fair skin deep beneath what my mirror reflected?

But my colour didn't seem to matter here. No one had seen my parents, so they couldn't compare their complexion to mine. I didn't have to make any effort to look a certain way like I did back home with the talcum powder. I understood what freedom tastes like – chicken curry for a so-called vegetarian. I devoured chicken curry, wore my colour with confidence, and danced all I wanted, unfettered.

Previously unwilling to push myself or participate in any

activities, I embraced everything that was on offer. Besides, days would have passed by like decades if I had resisted. I found my calling. Boxing lessons were a part of the morning activities. It was time for me to shine among a strong group of. . .two participants. One boy and I had enrolled; the boy proved to be inept. I was hooked right from the first jab, dreaming of becoming the first Indian female boxer. Boxing, in many ways, was like dancing with aggression. It required muscle memory, a set of choreographed moves, a touch of improvisation, and lots of pent-up anger. There was no shortage there. If anything, it was difficult to work out what angered me most: bedwetting, my colour, the feeling of abandonment, or my shattered dream of becoming a Bollywood actress.

I used all that rage in my lessons. The result: the trainer ended up with a slight bleed from his jelly-like nose. He had been some sort of champion and won a few matches, during which his nose ended up being the punch bag for his opponents. He left days after the nosebleed simply because there weren't enough takers for the sport; I boasted that his departure was due to embarrassment.

So, I tried my luck at another exotic sport: horse riding. A captivating female chestnut horse visited twice a week. She flaunted an unblemished, chocolate-brown body and a black mane and tail. I could stand in the vast dirt field watching her gallop for hours. Her body glistened with every graceful step, and her tail danced.

I was a fast learner; several teachers had told me that. I quickly learned how to mount on the saddle and how to control the horse with the reins. One morning, overexcited and overconfident, I nudged her with my right foot a little too hard. She went galloping off, full steam ahead. The instructor yelled from far behind, 'Pull the reins!' Of course, I would have done that if I could. But the reins were out of my hands. I was so frightened of her speeding up that I voluntarily fell off a galloping horse. It was a risk I was willing to take. My prize was a few deep gashes and a sprained ankle. Back to the bucket with hot water and salt.

That wasn't the end of my escapades with unusual sports. There was one more – archery – before I finally resorted to more conservative choices. I tried it. Didn't like it. Quit. My routine was set with all sorts of other activities, until the day a devastating event rocked the nation.

In October of that year, Prime Minister Indira Gandhi was assassinated by two of her trusted Sikh bodyguards. Tension in the country had been building up because Sikhs had been protesting for an independent state, Khalistan, for months. These protests had caused some bloodshed, both among Hindus and Sikhs. On 1 June 1984, Indira Gandhi ordered the Indian Army to remove the Sikh leader, Jarnail Singh Bhindranwale, from the Golden Temple in Punjab. This angered the Sikhs as they saw this as an attack on their religion, the Golden Temple being their holiest site.

Indira Gandhi's assassination on 31 October 1984 was a retaliatory act. She was showered by bullets within moments of stepping out of her bungalow. The news sent shockwaves across the entire country, sparking riots immediately. Government figures claimed that over the next three days, up to 3,000 Sikhs were killed, the victims of mass anger. Other sources reported 8,000 deaths or more.[3] The capital city, Delhi, suffered the most from the massacre, bearing witness to hideous crimes. I was, of course, oblivious to all this, sheltered in my boarding school. To this day, however,

I wonder why our school thought it was a good idea to go on a scheduled day trip, around a week later, with a few other schools. I cannot remember where.

What happened next lives in my memory as a faint but chilling incident, although it involved ferocious flames. There are gaps, complete blackouts. There are nebulous recollections, as though everything happened on a dark, thunderous night with flashes of lightning casting just enough light to see intermittently. And then there are a few vivid, terrifying fragments.

Dusk appeared on the horizon as we made our journey back to school. Vehicles had just switched on their headlights. We were dropping off some other children at their boarding school first. As soon as the teachers got up from the front row of the coach and turned to us, we noticed their horrified faces staring into the distance through the back windshield of the coach. I don't remember how many teachers were with us or what they looked like. I only remember commands. We all turned, curious to see what had them transfixed. A sea of bright, dancing flames. The flames appeared to grow larger every few seconds. They were, in fact, dozens of torches, not buildings set ablaze as we had initially presumed. Within moments, silhouettes of human forms appeared as dark shadows beneath the torches. A large mob was heading towards us, the commotion as horrifying as the flames. Such mobs were common during the riots.

A few days before this trip, we had picked up some harrowing stories from teachers who had exchanged news of the riots in the canteen.

'The Hindus are so bloodthirsty, they are dragging Sikh

men out of their homes and burning them alive. They aren't even sparing children, especially boys,' said one teacher.

'Inhumane!' said the other. 'And they are looting the *izzat*, honour, of Sikh women.' I didn't know what that meant then: rape.

Back on the bus, the teachers' trepidation got the better of them, arguing about the next step for what seemed like an eternity. Stay in the bus, duck low, and hide in the gaps between the seats? Or seek cover in the boarding school across the road? On seeing some children become hysterical, one teacher finally took charge, 'Everyone, leave the bus. Now!'

I disagreed. I preferred to hide in the coach. But what did a seven-year-old know? It was just as well I didn't have the authority to make pressing life decisions then. Between fight, flight, or hide (my preferred option), the decision was made for all of us to flee, and we complied.

I wasn't sure why I followed the teachers – the fear of getting ambushed, or the desire to stay close to the rest, despite disagreeing with their choice. In such life-and-death situations, fear and security become inseparably intertwined, both equal driving factors in deciding to follow the flock. Which we did, like little ducklings.

With time racing against us, numbness and confusion gripped me. I stopped midway, turning to the right to witness the power of this angry mob. Never mind the flames, their fury was enough to burn us alive. A warm orange hue around the mob, beautiful and hypnotic but still deathly, anchored me. Then, as the rest moved further away, the fear of separation took charge. I ran the fastest I have ever run. My life was in danger and fleeing was the only option.

'Are they going to burn us alive, Miss?' I asked one of the teachers, wishing I wasn't there. I wanted Mummy and Papa to be there to quell my fears, to hold my hand, more than ever. I yearned for the safety of their arms.

'Shhh, don't stop! Stay with us!'

'I want Mummy.' I quivered and reached for the teacher's hand. But she was already holding onto another child. I grabbed the sari hanging behind her left shoulder.

We made it to the other side, barged into any open rooms, and turned off all the lights. I don't remember seeing other children or teachers in the rooms as though everyone else was invisible. In those few minutes, the sun had set entirely, but the streetlights hadn't yet come on. Even the light from the flames hadn't reached us yet. Trembling in the dark, we followed every command from our teachers. They undraped the turbans of the Sikh boys among us, looking out of the window every few seconds. The girls were instructed to rummage through all cupboards and look for any spare dresses. Petrified, I didn't move from my spot.

'Hurry up! We haven't got much time!' whispered one teacher, peering outside, seeing the mob closing in. We could hear their roar.

To transform the boys into girls, the teachers let loose their hair and pull dresses over their clothes.

'That's not enough!' said another teacher. She reached out for a pair of scissors in an open drawer. How she managed to spot a pair, in the dark, in such an emergency, I don't know. She snipped the hair of some of the Sikh boys in one quick motion. A blasphemous liberty. All squirmed but none objected. With a variety of hair lengths, it became harder to distinguish the Sikh boys. Even the most perceptive attackers would be thrown off.

The last instruction from the lead teacher to us was, 'If they come in, grab you, and ask you for your name, don't say a word! Nothing at all, we will do the talking.' We all understood why. Sikh names gave away their identity immediately. I felt relieved for those boys. Their gender, appearance, hair and name, their entire identity had been altered within minutes. They were in safe hands.

Before we all darted and sought shelter under beds, one of the teachers chopped her knee-length plait off. She was Sikh.

The boys looked pretty dressed as girls. They looked more like girls than I did with my bob haircut. Suddenly, I panicked. If those rioters out there, thirsty for blood, laid their eyes on me they would think I was a boy. I had more of a chance of being slain than the boys themselves. If there were ever a time to wet myself justifiably, this would have been it! I thought I was going to die. Alone.

Then, as I lay crouched under a bed, another thought extinguished the panic. I looked like a boy but not like any Sikh boy with us. They were all milky white. So were the Sikh girls. In my enclosed world at boarding school, Sikhs were the fairest, scoring 1 on the Fairometer. I hadn't seen any other colour on them. Deducing that all Sikhs were fair, I felt out of danger, no longer a possible target. The last thing I remember is shutting my eyes and muttering, 'Mummy.'

The lights went out then. Complete darkness. Except the lights were never turned on. It was the lights in my mind. After I was comforted by the thought of my colour being my saviour, every detail of the incident from that moment on was lost forever. I can't remember if the mob raided the building, we managed to fool them, and they left disappointed having not found any Sikh boys. I can't remember if we stayed the night there, falling asleep under those beds. I suppose if there were any injuries or deaths, I would have retained those memories. Therefore, I assume we all made it out safely.

For once, I was thankful for my colour. But, whether I liked it or not, colour was at the forefront of my mind again. It spun back like a boomerang, creeping in without any notice when I had been working hard to eradicate such thoughts. Even worse, this was the start of preconceptions I held about certain communities being of a certain complexion. And if colour and community go hand in hand, my community was my family.

Obsessing about colour, I returned to the niggling question. Why was my colour different and how could I get back to my 'original' shade?

9

THE BLACK ROSE

March 1985, India

I caught chickenpox. Despite a high temperature and itchy spots scattered all over my body (even inside the left ear), I had reason to rejoice because all pupils with the illness were quarantined in a different room for two weeks. It was a holiday from Payal.

Sheetal and I were best friends, attached at the hip except when she ran faster than me. At the same time, the cold war between Payal and me was escalating to an unbearable level, which egged her on to shower me with more taunts daily. So I built a wall around myself as protection from her ridicule, and her remarks started to fall on deaf ears. Back in Kobe, we had visited a doctor to treat my bedwetting, but over a month in, the medication hadn't worked. Every night I used the toilet by myself, sparing Mummy a trip to accompany me. She noticed the effort. But here I was, still bedwetting daily. And now, I wasn't just washing my own sheet.

'Since you're doing the laundry, you can wash my clothes for me too,' Payal used to say, leaving a pile for me. I obliged.

For two weeks in quarantine, I didn't have to wash her clothes. Around a dozen of us slept on mattresses lined up on the floor in Room 1. This room felt smaller and darker, although it was the same size as Room 11. Those dozen bodies seemed to absorb more light from the room.

The first few days were a welcome change but then, as any ill child does, I started to miss my parents. As soon as they came to know, the matron allowed me to speak to them on the phone. Just as well, or else I would have had to wait until I recovered and made the next fortnightly visit to Nani's. And if the two didn't coincide, it could be a month before I would be able to speak to Mummy and Papa.

After I recovered, Papa surprised me with a flying visit, even though the summer holiday was only two months away. I showed him around with pride, baffled by this emotion. I had thought that I didn't like it here, yet my tour of the school affirmed that I did. There was no doubt it was an outstanding facility in the 1980s. I also knew that coming from our humble background, it was a big financial stretch for my parents. When Papa used to work in a factory, I owned a total of three dresses, attended a state school, and we never ate out. Mummy had once told me that there were days my parents scrimped on food. 'We used to run out of the monthly salary regularly. One of the months when I was expecting you, both your father and I survived on one mango a day for a week,' she said.

Moving from a frugal life to a state-of-the-art boarding school, along with all the goodies from Japan, started to make me feel grateful. Even so, my emotions were a pendulum. One moment I was full to the brim with gratitude, the next minute I was at rock bottom, feeling abandoned, desperate to be united with my family. Luckily for Papa, on the day he visited I felt the former.

I escorted him to my room, caught sight of Payal, and gulped. Since I had moved back into the room after quarantine, my indifference to her remarks was bothering her. I was still in 'chickenpox holiday bliss'. She must have been bottling up a surplus of abusive comments for two weeks, with no one to spew on. And when she finally got a chance, I can't imagine a worse feeling than receiving no reaction.

There wasn't much to show to Papa. The room wasn't exactly a five-star retreat. There were four beds, some shelves above the beds, chipped, whitewashed walls, and the shared damp bathroom.

Payal's eyes followed Papa, tracing every step. I had learned to read her face. She had questions. She had things to say. My left palm, the one stuck to Papa's palm, started sweating.

Keep your mouth shut. He already knows about my bedwetting.

I had grown accustomed to the abuse but wasn't prepared to tolerate being the cause of embarrassment to Papa.

'That's all there is. Let me show you my classroom,' I pulled his hand, dragging him out before Payal could slip in any nasty words. But instead of heading to my classroom, Papa led the way to the matron's office. 'Let's get permission for you to come with me to Karol Bagh for the night,' he said. It wasn't yet the end of the month when we could go home for a family visit. The matron's mood, as varied as the four seasons, was generous and giving that spring. I sprinted back to my room, stuffed my pyjamas in a bag, and dashed back to the office.

At Nani's, all the aunts and uncles surrounded Papa, wanting to pamper him. The family treated their son-in-law like royalty. I didn't want to leave his side but there wasn't any room for me among all the adults.

'Have a look in Nani's room. I've brought something for you,' Papa said. He knew I wanted all his attention, but he had to give a share to the in-laws.

On Nani's bed lay a big plastic bag from Daiei, a Japanese department store. Gift wrapping and ribbons were also not a thing in our family. There was no fuss over presents, which were rare in any case. I shoved my hand into the bag, opened it wider, and rummaged through the items. Another Hello Kitty nightie and a white dress with layers of netting underneath, like a princess frock. Grinning, I thanked Papa and slipped into the dress. He was still surrounded by family, so I tagged along with an aunt heading to the kitchen to make tea. She asked me to serve it to an elderly man in the living room.

This man was Nana's best friend; he visited for a tea break daily from his shop of Indian accessories opposite the family restaurant. He stood six feet tall, very tall for an Indian man in those days. He had a deep, hostile voice, and his features were so sharp, they looked unnatural. Like a man-witch. A white *kurta* and white *dhoti*, tied in a manner that resembled loose trousers, softened his foreboding aura. I never understood why my Nana was close to him, honouring him with the title of 'the best friend'. I called him The Wicked Man.

I edged towards the living room, balancing the full cup of tea and saucer in both hands. He took a quick glance. 'This tea is too weak. Look at its colour. Go and tell your aunt to brew it for longer. I want it as dark as the colour of your skin,' he said, pushing the cup and saucer away. I stared at him, hoping that if I stared long enough my wrath would burn him.

'Go!' he barked. 'What are you looking at?'

'Papa!' My cry for help didn't reach him although he was in the neighbouring room. As usual, the noise level there had reached a saturation point.

'Papa? Go ask your Papa where you got your colour from!' The Wicked Man grabbed my wrist hard, making it impossible to wriggle out. Some tea spilt into the saucer and onto my new dress. 'Your Mummy and Papa are ashamed of your colour. That's why they have left you here.'

'That's not true! They love me!'

I bit his hand and scurried out, spilling more tea on the way back to the kitchen. I cried harder on seeing the tea stains on my dress. After telling the aunt to make some more tea, I vanished and hid in Sona Mami's room until The Wicked Man left.

When Sangeeta Mausi returned from college, I told her about The Wicked Man.

'Don't let it bother you, *beta*. He says such things to me too,' she said.

'He does? Like what?'

'He says I look like a Madrasi.'

'What is that?'

'South Indians. They generally have darker skin like us.'

'Why does he make fun of our skin when *his* colour is not any different to ours?'

'You're right, it isn't. But he's a man. It's very different for men,' said Mausi, drawing me in for a hug. 'Now, did I tell you how beautiful you look in that dress? Like a fairy. Take it off and I'll wash off those tea stains for you.'

The aroma of sweet *halwa* was a perfect wake-up call the next morning. Papa and I feasted on a heavy breakfast followed by *halwa* and then left for school. He was quiet on the way there, short of jokes, short of conversation. I too spent most of the journey gazing out of the taxi window, hiding my tears, analysing what The Wicked Man had said. I didn't think that he would have the answer to my daily question - *Why am I here?* - lying in my rickety, metal-frame bed in Room 11.

It's not the smoking. It's not the bedwetting. Education is an excuse. I am in a boarding school because of my colour.

This thought tortured me. To distract myself, I started reading the number plates of vehicles passing by, until the thought crept in again. When we approached the black gates, I welled up and clung to Papa's arm, begging him to take me with him.

'Why do you leave me here, Papa? Why can't I live with you like Neeraj? Am I here because you're ashamed of me?'

'What? Who said that to you?!' Papa exclaimed. He leaned to hug me. 'Why would we ever be ashamed of you? Mummy and I are proud of you, our strong little girl.'

'No one.' I fidgeted with his watch. I wanted him to ask me again. I wanted attention. If he did, I would have told him. But he missed the signs. So, I put on a brave face, punishing myself.

He sighed, avoiding eye contact. 'A few more weeks and you'll be home for the summer. Remember how much fun you had on the plane journey all by yourself?'

Home for the summer. A permanent move was not on the cards. Papa knew that the plane ride was a lame attempt at consoling me, but I suppose he had nothing better. Then he opened up, unlike most Indian men reluctant to share their emotions and insecurities with anybody, let alone with a seven-year-old child.

'I'm working very hard for your admission into a school in Kobe. As soon as I can make enough money, you'll be with us.'

'The one with the blue-and-white-striped uniform?' I asked.

'Yes, that one,' he smiled, wiping my tears.

I remembered how much my chest hurt the first time my father dropped me off. It hurt less this time. He was doing everything in his capacity to transfer me. Silence was already an attribute I had learned to master. Now it was time to master patience.

I returned to the room by myself because the matron didn't allow Papa to take me. Payal was waiting to pounce on me. The cat had caught a glimpse of the mouse.

Great. What are you going to strike with now?

'That man who was here yesterday, who was he?'

'My Papa.'

'Ha, he can't be.'

'What do you mean? He *is* my father.'

'Yeah sure, and mine is Amitabh Bachchan,' she scoffed,

referring to the Bollywood movie star. 'You don't look anything like the man with you. He's *gora-chitta* and you, *kali*.'

I knew that already, but her words still punctured me deeply. Once again, I chose silence as a way of ending the artillery firing at me. I sat on my bed, sobbing and scanning the room for Sheetal. She wasn't there. I cried until I ran out of tears and fell asleep.

Shaking my left shoulder rather forcefully, Sheetal woke me up. 'Shweta, come on, we haven't got much time.'

'For what?' My eyes were still shut.

'The school has arranged a visit to the garden this afternoon. Get ready, it'll be fun. We must meet by the steps of the main building in five minutes.'

'Is she coming?' I mouthed, glancing at Payal in the room. Sheetal shook her head.

There wasn't much to do to get ready. I shoved my feet into my white trainers, my heels creasing the backs, and off we both went. A handful of us showed up at the steps and we followed the teacher, sauntering and chatting a little too much for her liking.

'Stop chatting and hurry up. I haven't got the rest of the afternoon to chaperone you all to the garden,' she chided.

The garden, by the entrance of the school, was a five-minute walk. Spring was blooming in its full glory. There were flowers everywhere, bursting with colour and ambrosial scents. It wasn't so much a well-maintained garden, more like a field of wildflowers haphazardly planted, but it was a haven in the austere compound. The earthy smell of the moist soil relaxed me. I strolled through the garden, inhaling deep breaths. Having to wash my white trainers after returning from the garden was never a chore. Mud-stained trainers were a reminder of fresh air and freedom in the true sense.

A little deeper in the field, a crotchety gardener was plucking out some roses, past a patch of sunflowers taller than me. He looked fatigued. He had been gardening all day and was unhappy about children disturbing him, delaying his journey home. As we approached him, the teacher started questioning him about the life cycle of roses. His mood changed. He found the energy to stand taller, to boast about his knowledge of all flowers. He continued plucking out the half-bloomed, crimson roses, pointing to various other patches of flowers when discussing them. Still plucking and talking, he skipped a rose.

'Why have you left this rose?' I asked.

'Its colour is not right,' he huffed, uninterested in entertaining my question.

'What do you mean, not right?' I wasn't going to drop this.

'It's a little too dark. See, the others in my basket are a brighter shade of maroon. This one is darker with a touch of black. It won't look right in my bunch.'

Before all the surrounding roses were plucked, this 'black' rose stood out, proud of its uniqueness. Now left destitute, it appeared feeble in its solitary existence.

Through no fault of its own, the rose was deemed undesirable for not conforming to the norm. The gardener's opinion was based on its colour; it wasn't as beautiful because it was a darker shade.

That rose resonated with me in more ways than I can

describe. It was different in its rosebush. I was different in my family. And people around me didn't hesitate to remind me. My complexion didn't match the rest of my family's, that was undeniable. But was it such a punishable crime to be different from them? Like the rose, was this the real reason for my exclusion from my family? I couldn't help but wonder whether The Wicked Man was right, whether I was The Black Rose.

10

MISFIT

May 1986, Japan

The Black Rose is my last vivid memory of Virendra Gram Boarding School. Everything from March 1985 to June 1986 is a total void. Hopelessly lost.

After two years and four months at the boarding school, I was finally reunited with my family. Yet I don't remember the anticipation, the expected euphoria at the reunion. Nor do I remember bidding farewell to the black gates, Sheetal, Karol Bagh, or India. Sangeeta Mausi's wedding and the plane ride with my family don't come to mind either. But I will never forget my reaction to being told that Sangeeta Mausi was getting married.

'Stop following her around,' said Maya Mami. 'Kallo will be married in June and will leave the house.'

My eyes pooled with tears.

'I can't live without you, *and* Mummy and Papa,' I wailed in Sangeeta Mausi's lap. 'Can I live with you after you get married?'

She wiped my tears, alternating her gentle stroke between one cheek and the other. 'I wish I could take you with me, *beta.* You know, your Mummy and Papa are coming for the wedding?'

'So what? They'll come, spend some time here, bring me lots of gifts, and go back. I can't live without you, Mausi.'

'I know you're upset but they love you dearly. And guess what? You'll be going home with them. Forever!'

'I will?' The tears stopped instantaneously.

The next thing I remember is waking up next to Neeraj. Crickets up in the mountains chirped almost as loud as my heavy breathing. My chest burned with pain as though I had run all the way from the boarding school to Kobe. I had a nightmare in which I was standing behind the black gates. I wanted to get out but had no strength to push them open. I wanted to run back to the boarding school, but my feet were anchored to the ground. Everything around me was dark; the shadow of The Black Rose draped the boarding school as though it was upset with me for leaving.

Despite now living in Kobe, this nightmare made frequent visits. Although Papa had confirmed my admission at a school, I still suspected that I was a temporary visitor, that I would be catching the same flight back to India when the summer break was over. Call it managing expectations, not being too hopeful, or perhaps The Wicked Man's words preying on my fears.

I was now going to attend St Michael's International School. Its exterior was brilliant white, as though the sky in Kobe had another invisible sun dedicated to smiling solely on the school. Colourful artwork filled every inch of wall space in the corridors, and the playground looked inviting, unlike the vast, empty field of the boarding school.

A short stroll from home and a minute from Baskin Robbins, the school was a dream location for a fourth-grader. September 1986, on my first walk to the school, dressed in the blue-and-white-striped uniform, and clenching Mummy's hand, I murmured to myself, 'I'm home.'

That evening, when Papa came home, Neeraj scurried toward him before me. 'Papa hoshi,' he said, wrapping his arms around Papa's leg. Like I used to. I peeled his arms off our father's leg. He started crying and bit my hand. I went straight for his hair. He wailed and pulled my hair.

'He's your little brother, Shweta,' Papa said, standing in between us. Neeraj took shelter behind him. I wanted to tell Papa that no one talked to me on my first day at school, but Neeraj started again with his chant, 'Papa hoshi,' his arms outstretched, asking Papa to pick him up.

Neeraj had stopped sleepwalking, but 'Papa hoshi' was still his mantra. Papa had another fan, adding a new dimension to our sibling rivalry. A four-year-old and a nine-year-old competing for their father's attention. As Neeraj already had Mummy's attention, it was only fair that he left Papa's for me. Our relationship hadn't been a rosy one to begin with. From then on, it only worsened. Scratching faces and pulling hair became our standard greeting within minutes of laying our eyes on each other.

Kanika became my first friend at school. Although she looked nothing like Sheetal, she was Sheetal with a mischievous edge, a gregarious girl with enormous eyes as black as her hair. Unlike other pretty girls in the class, Kanika was kind. Our complexions occupied the opposite ends of the Fairometer, but my colour was the least of her concerns.

Every day we would walk to and from school together, often ending up at her house. Informing Mummy of my whereabouts was usually an afterthought. Our ideal playdate was dressing up and dancing to Madonna's *Papa Don't Preach*. Sometimes we would prank-call boys, all from her own bedroom. I couldn't reciprocate with such playdates in our one-bedroom apartment.

Kanika remodelled me. She refined my taste buds and introduced me to world cuisine like pizza and pasta. Anything other than Indian food was *world cuisine*. The makeover made little difference in impressing the rest of my classmates. My Indian accent, Indian lunch boxes, sense of fashion, and broken English – the entire package – made me a misfit. I enrolled in activities to become an integral part of the class. Playing the recorder, the flute, attending Brownies, baking, I did it all. No team sports, of course, as I quickly realised I would be the last one standing in the school playground when team leaders selected their players.

If there was anything I shunned, it was extra English lessons. I was impressed with my broken English until Mrs Smithson's lunchtime class when even a broken sentence wouldn't pass my lips. Her polished British accent added to the challenge. On hearing her speak, I would lose my words. Most of the time she had to repeat the instructions before I understood tasks as simple as, 'Read a paragraph from this book today.' I started with the *Biff, Chip and Kipper* series and daydreamed through most of the sessions, a drag for her as much as they were for me.

Mrs Smithson didn't fall for any of my mundane excuses, such as, 'I need to go to the toilet.' However, I once pulled off 'The headmaster wants to see me after lunch,' well. She excused me.

That evening, when I lay in bed sandwiched between Papa and Mummy, my father asked, 'Why does Mrs Smithson want to see us, Shweta?'

I said nothing, biting my nails. Papa caught my eyes travelling to a novel on his bedside table, *A Stranger in the Mirror* by Sidney Sheldon. Seldom did Papa not have a book. I used to shudder, flicking through his thick novels with fine text. Mummy always had a stack of Hindi novels by her bedside too.

'I hate reading.' I sat up, my arms crossed, gazing out the window. 'I can't read all the words and my classmates make fun of me.'

'All the *more* reason to read. You must practise to improve. When I was a little boy, my family was very poor. Our village's school didn't have any English teachers, let alone English books. I learned how to read with newspaper scraps littering the streets. I read under our streetlights because our house didn't have electricity. We had kerosene lamps back then, only used in the kitchen for cooking.'

His childhood stories of how he steered his own fate by educating himself were both inspirational and daunting. 'Reading also improves your vo-ca-bul-ry. I still...'

'Not *vo-ca-bul-ry*. It's *voh-ca-b-uw-lary*,' I corrected him, seizing the opportunity to boast. 'Even *I* know that.' If there was any word I had mastered the pronunciation of, it was *vocabulary*. Mrs Smithson had been drilling the same message into me.

'Yes, that. I still learn new words.'

He never quite got the pronunciation of the word right. But his insatiable hunger for knowledge was endearing. I could never match that. Papa learned by reading. I learned by talking, for which I often got into trouble. Talking, albeit inarticulately, was my priority to make friends and practise speaking English. The one unanimous complaint in my quarterly school report – that I was 'quite a chatterbox and often distracts her classmates' – was no deterrent.

During the entire first year at the school, I shadowed Kanika, waiting to be accepted. Persistent attempts at fitting in were exhausting. Before we broke for the summer, a dental company came in for a routine annual check-up arranged by the school. We were all asked to take a sip of some purple syrup, rinse our mouths with it for 30 seconds, and then spit it out. It left a sticky, metallic taste in the mouth, like when you've eaten one too many cherries. The colouring from the syrup was an indicator of your oral health. The darker the residue on your teeth, the poorer your brushing technique.

One by one, the dentist checked all our teeth as we lined up with our purple-tainted mouths wide open.

'*Ha kirei ne, Shweta chan,*' said the dentist. I turned to Kanika beside me for the translation.

'Your teeth are clean,' she said.

'I can get a double scoop of chocolate-chip ice cream today, then,' I whispered.

After that, the dentist didn't praise anyone else. Our homeroom teacher, Mrs Tanaka, asked me, 'Can you help me hand out the dental care sheets to the class? Seems like you have the cleanest and the whitest teeth here.'

At last, a triumphant moment after an entire year at school, climbing a mountain of struggles. I didn't think my teeth would pave the path to popularity. I found myself daydreaming again – a daydream in which everyone wanted me on their team. What do good teeth have anything to do with sports teams? Nothing. I was only nine and still entitled to nonsensical daydreams.

I rushed to the teacher's desk to grab the handouts.

'It's the only thing white on her body,' a familiar voice from behind remarked. It was Nikhil. His baby face, one that used to get away with a thousand mischiefs before trouble touched him, mismatched his wittiness. Our mothers often ended up in each other's apartments for a cup of tea. On the odd occasion when I had to tag along with Mummy, Nikhil wouldn't entertain me. He kept himself occupied with Super Mario games and homework. Classmates had started teasing Nikhil and me like we were dating. Maybe that was the reason for his indignant remarks in school – to prove otherwise.

Laughter filled the classroom. I was used to such laughter at boarding school, a full classroom mocking me for bedwetting, but this was the first time a classroom full of children laughed at my colour. This hurt far more. I maintained my steady pace towards Mrs Tanaka's desk, determined not to turn around.

The next afternoon, Mrs Smithson entered the classroom for our English period, swinging a book and several photocopied sheets in her left hand. We were facing yet another reading session. I buried my head in my arms on my desk. She shuffled to the teacher's desk, dressed in a buttoned-up, round-neck white blouse, and a long, grey skirt. As she sat down, putting on her glasses suspended from a necklace, the room went quiet. If it weren't for a volunteer handing out the photocopies, we could have heard the sea waves crashing against Kobe Port fifteen minutes away. That was the kind of attention Mrs Smithson commanded.

I still had my head down when I heard a ruffling of papers as the volunteer placed a photocopy on my desk. I looked at the title. Before I could read it, Mrs Smithson read out loud, '*The Ugly Duckling* by Hans Christian Andersen. Who would like to start with the first paragraph?'

Plenty of eager hands went up, mine excluded. I would be inviting trouble, reading aloud in class in an accent that was amusing to others. Students took turns reading one paragraph each until we finally reached the last paragraph. The end, thank goodness. I wasn't called upon to read anything. The moment the bell rang, there was a commotion in the classroom. Everyone was talking over each other while packing their bags.

Kanika waited by my desk. As we approached the door together, a voice called, 'Hey, Shweta, why didn't you read any part of the story?' I turned to see Angad, taking long strides towards me, which used to puzzle me as he was the shortest boy in the class. He also wore glasses with lenses so thick, they may as well have been magnifying glasses.

'Is it because it's *your* story? Because *you're* the ugly duckling in your family?' he said.

'Shut up, Angad!' Kanika defended me. 'Have you seen *yourself* in the mirror?'

'I have. I look like my family. Have you seen hers? She *is* the ugly duckling in hers,' smirked Angad.

After a whole year of dropping my guard, colour-related comments were back with a vengeance. Although Angad was my colour, I had no counterargument to his taunt. Going by stereotypical definitions of beauty, whether in the animal kingdom or in our human world, I was the odd one out. The Ugly Duckling in my family.

This was my story, but with one caveat: the ugly duckling had the last laugh, turning into a beautiful swan. I didn't see that metamorphosis in my future.

11
MIRROR, MIRROR

Summer of 1988, India

Not all insults were colour-related and not all came from The Boys – mainly Angad and Nikhil. Sometimes, other boys joined in from other classes during recess or lunch breaks. The taunts about my skin tone were so monotonous that hearing jibes about anything else, and from anyone else, felt refreshing.

'Why aren't you coming on that day trip?' asked Katherine, the golden-haired, blue-eyed, most popular girl in class. 'Because your father can't pay for it?'

I told Papa and within days he arranged to pay for the day trip.

'I always see your mother walking everywhere. Doesn't your family have a car? Are you that poor?' said Elizabeth, swinging on the monkey bars during recess. She always wore her light brown hair in a high ponytail.

For months I pestered Papa about getting a car, every evening over dinner and every Sunday after his bath.

'We can't now but we will soon,' he would say. Unbeknown to us, he had a peculiar fear of sitting behind the wheel. He shielded his weaknesses from us. This irrational fear of driving (given that he used to ride a scooter in India) gave Mummy and me a good excuse to tease him. His fear wasn't abating anytime soon, so Mummy volunteered to learn to drive. Carrying shopping bags uphill had started to cause debilitating pain in her shoulders and arms. I was surprised she had waited so long. Getting a car was imperative then. Not straight away, but at least it was on the cards.

'Everyone in our class has their own bedroom except you,' said Sharon, pushing her red glasses up, after I invited her for a playdate.

The same year, we moved to a larger two-bedroom apartment, which was still within walking distance of the school. Neeraj and I shared a bunk bed, with me claiming the top tier. I still didn't have my own bedroom, but I thought that all these changes would bring me acceptance in the class. They helped, but The Boys had clocked my weakness, my single most paralysing pressure point. And whenever they were in the mood to tease me, they stuck to one theme.

In the summer of 1988, I visited Delhi with my family. It was a much-needed break from the unpleasant comments throughout the year. But expecting a break from skin-colour obsession while in India was foolhardy. The notion stalked me.

A particular whitening cream had made its home in every corner shop on every street. Beauty parlours offered tan-removing and skin-whitening facials. My aunts applied homemade face and body masks regularly, made with gram flour, yoghurt, and lemon juice to remove their tan. Bollywood movies glamorised fairer skin. Among a dozen

A-list actresses, there was one dark-skinned actress at the time, Smita Patil. It was a shame I only came to know of her after her death in 1986, after which I watched a few of her movies and felt proud seeing her on screen.

Maya Mami was wrong. There *was* a dark-skinned actress making waves. Then I realised, there *was* only *one*.

Around this time, I also noticed a lot of songs addressed the actresses as *gori* or *goriya*. The lyrics of one song, which was stuck in my head, were: 'Don't step out in the sun, oh queen of beauty. Your fair colour might turn *kala*.' Actor Amitabh Bachchan danced behind the actress, holding an umbrella up for her. Ironically, the actress wasn't *gori*. The song enraged me, yet I hummed it all the time.

Worst of all, arranged marriage proposals came with biodatas (essentially a personal profile) that included a reference to skin tone, based on the four descriptions on the Fairometer. This seemed to be a requirement for females yet voluntary for males. How did I know this as a ten-year-old? I happened to eavesdrop on a conversation at a sari store with Mummy. Two female friends, browsing through dozens of saris for their wedding, were discussing how they cheated with their photographs. Excessive lighting and lighter foundation took their Fairometer reading one level higher than their actual tone. When potential suitors visited, they were questioned about their colour. But by then they had managed to woo them enough to send a proposal.

It wasn't just women who obsessed over fair skin. The Wicked Man still visited daily, still dressed head to toe in white. I managed to avoid him most days but not for long. Once again, I was asked to serve him tea as he sat in the same chair in the living room. The incident from last year flashed before my eyes. Maybe he had had a bad day. He was Nana's best friend; he couldn't have been all evil. I changed my mind when I saw his nefarious smile as soon as I walked into the room. Prey approaching predator. He grabbed my wrist again.

'You must be very happy to be living in Japan with them,' he said.

I wriggled. He tightened his grip, hurting me. I yielded like a culprit in handcuffs.

What does he mean by 'them'?

'You don't belong there. Your brother does. Because he belongs to them. But you, can't you see you are not their daughter.'

'I am! And they are my Mummy and Papa! Even more than Neeraj's! I was born first.'

'Neeraj looks like them. You don't look anything like them. They found you on their doorstep. Haven't they told you yet? Look at you, skinny and *kali*, like Chotu. Like a homeless beggar's child on the street. They raised you, taking pity on you. Then when it came to moving to Japan, they left you here. Think about it – why didn't they leave Neeraj here?'

A Beggar's Child. Another 'B'.

'Because he was a baby. They couldn't leave him here.'

'That's what they have told you. Your aunts and uncles looked after you. Why couldn't they look after Neeraj? Your parents chose to take Neeraj with them because he *is* their son.'

I bawled, choking on my tears. The more I cried, the wider his smile grew, imbued with satisfaction.

'So what? I'm with them now!' I cried for help, but no one was around mid-afternoon. Mummy was out for a driving lesson; Papa was in the family restaurant. In Delhi's mid-August scorching heat, everyone else had retired to their rooms for a nap.

I can't remember any more of the pernicious conversation. Nor can I remember how long The Wicked Man carried on with his poisonous words. I zoned out, sobbing. When he finally let go, I ran barefoot up three flights of stairs to the roof terrace. The soles of my feet burned on the hot stone staircase. I hid, and to torment myself, I replayed the conversation again and again in my mind. His words spun around me, bringing my whole world tumbling down, warped and sucked into darkness.

Why would a trusted adult say such things? And if he did, there must be some truth to it. Being an orphan would explain the drastic colour difference. But Mummy and Papa never differentiated between Neeraj and me. I knew they loved me. Why didn't I say that? If I were not their child, why would they bother bringing me to Kobe? They could have left me in the boarding school for eternity, to be raised by teachers, aunts, uncles, and Sheetal.

Eventually, I concluded that this man unveiled his vile side only to me. He gave me a ticket to a private show, a seat reserved for one. He had everyone else dancing to his tune at a completely different show. His words wounded me, deeply; invisible wounds that I didn't reveal to anyone, not even to my parents. A part of me had started believing there must be a grain of truth in The Wicked Man's jibes. I didn't have the courage to investigate and face my findings. Moreover, words from a child usually held no weight compared to a respected elder. I decided to carry the canker with me, letting it fester. If only I had known that The Wicked Man would continue with his remarks every time he saw me, his favourite being, 'a beggar's child' and 'they found you on their doorstep.' I lost count of how many times he grabbed me that summer.

By comparison, remarks from The Boys barely qualified as teasing. With us being the same age, there was a level playing field. I could handle ten months of occasional verbal abuse from classmates my age. At least I had a chance to talk back, even though I chose not to. It was preferable to two months of torture by an old man to whom I couldn't utter a word because it was a sign of disrespect in our culture. The Wicked Man and The Boys – the two walls were closing in on me. Standing up to either party had started to become a herculean task.

Fortunately, umpteen aunts and cousins distracted me as we gallivanted about the local streets, snacking on street food together. And when we weren't out and about, we would all convene in the favourite sitting room, the birthplace of wit, humour, and sarcasm. Laughter naturally followed.

We would fly kites on the roof terrace until dusk, cram into the Ambassador, at least 11 of us, and carry a picnic to India Gate. I'd tag along with my cousins as a third wheel on their playdates. We would play hide and seek in the three-storey townhouse, which harboured more nooks and crannies than I could count. Hide and seek was my favourite, of course – it involved staying out of the sun.

My least favourite was story time with Naina, Sona Mami's four-year-old daughter, who'd started attending school in July. I didn't want to look at a book let alone read one during the summer break. But Sona Mami's words were my command.

'Shweta, can you read a story to her?' she said one afternoon, cleaning up the shrine in her small wooden cupboard. She was about to start her prayers.

I turned to Naina, sitting cross-legged on the bed, both hands holding her chin, elbows resting on her knees. A spread of fairy-tale books lay in front of her. *Cinderella, Little Red Riding Hood, Snow White,* and *Jack and the Beanstalk.*

'This one,' Naina said, pointing to *Snow White.* Snow White and Naina weren't far apart. Skin as white as milk with a drop of Rooh Afza – a pink rosewater syrup – and rosy cheeks. When she was a baby, I used to call her the Cerelac Baby, an advertiser's dream. Naina beamed with excitement. Engrossed in the reading, her big, round eyes were fixated on the pages of the book. I read a line, then translated it into Hindi. When I flipped pages, the next line was, 'Mirror, mirror on the wall, who is the fairest of them all?' I read and stopped. 'Mirror, mirror on the wall, who's the fairest of them all?' I read again.

Reading this fairytale at boarding school four years earlier, one teacher had translated the word 'fairest' as *gori-chitti* (pasty white). When I read *Snow White* with Mrs Smithson last year, she said it meant 'the kindest and the most beautiful'.

Naina's eyes shifted from the book to my face, waiting for the translation. 'Who's the *kindest* and most beautiful of them all?' I said.

'Teacher says *gori-chitti,*' Naina replied, looking puzzled. 'Like me,' she added, smiling. Sona Mami stopped chanting her prayers, intending to take over the conversation.

'Tell your teacher that my English teacher said it means this, not *gori-chitti*.'

Sona Mami smiled at me and carried on with her prayers. I left the room feeling proud. But it only lasted a moment before confusion fogged my thoughts. That day, I had preached one thing but desired another: to be fairer myself. What did that make me? A lot had happened in four years. I was made aware of my colour and its 'limitations' while Naina, a four-year-old, was introduced to fair-skin privilege, the teacher telling her she was *gori-chitti*.

How many children are being taught to believe that fairest means gori-chitti? If this is being taught in primary school, how could I possibly put up a fight against it? Should I just forgive and forget? Accept it and never question it? Or should I fight?

To forgive and forget seemed like the wiser option. Striving for change seemed futile. Besides, although every colour-related experience and comment disgusted me, the desire for fairer skin brewed beneath it all. Was it wrong to want to look like my family?

But someone must fight. Why not me?

From this point on, I see-sawed between the two choices. If I chose to fight, I couldn't help but think my efforts would be in vain. If I chose to forgive and forget, I would experience such prejudicial taunts that I would be riled up, ready to fight.

The conundrum's grip was starting to tighten, like the grip of The Wicked Man. I can't remember when the seesaw decided to go on autopilot, taking control of my actions.

12

POT KETTLE

September 1988, Japan

When we returned to Kobe from our summer holiday and as we were offloading our suitcases from the airport bus, I noticed several Japanese ladies stroll past carrying umbrellas on a bright day. It reminded me of the song lyrics: 'Don't step out in the sun, oh queen of beauty. Your fair colour might turn *kala*.' I didn't know then that the obsession with fair skin was prevalent in Japan too, but not discussed as brusquely as in India. I also didn't know that a whole range of skin-whitening products – creams, lotions, and soaps – were widely sold in cosmetics stores there. I decided to fight.

In September 1988, I began a new year at St Michael's, but thankfully I was not a new student anymore. I was ready to take on any colour-related comments, mostly from The Boys. I am sure others must have said things too, but comments from The Boys hurt the most because they were Indian themselves, different shades of brown. I'd thought that I could stomach their comments when compared to The Wicked Man's bitter words. But every comment felt like an unexpected jab in a boxing match, aimed straight at the heart.

The Boys carried on with growing confidence, applying anything we learned in lessons to me, such as 'the black sheep' or 'the bad apple'. Some teachers cackled at their silly humour, which frequently egged them on until they would take things too far.

Seeing the teachers' indifference, my pathetic responses were: '*You're* the black sheep!' and '*You're* the bad apple.'

I had a lot more comebacks stocked in my head, but the words never made it out; they were stifled by The Wicked Man's taunt: 'They found you on their doorstep.' The thought of possibly being an adopted child filled me with gratitude and reminded me not to be a troublemaker. If teachers ever caught me in a fight, I could easily defend myself because I didn't say anything offensive other than throw their own words back at them.

But school playgrounds and social gatherings brought about different behaviours and responses. One Saturday, almost every Indian in Kobe gathered at The India Club for bingo night. The club was the community's hub to engage in cultural, religious, and social activities under one roof. By the end of several games, I had won a new, black-and-red BMX bicycle, the only time I have ever won anything. From the main hall, a narrow staircase led to the ground-floor foyer. I was rushing down with Papa to collect my bike when Angad came marching up.

Not today, not now. I won't let him get me today. Besides, he couldn't; Papa was with me. As our paths crossed, I should have read his sly smile as a warning.

'Well done, Shweta,' Angad said. Then looking up at

Papa, he nodded and greeted him.

Papa returned the greeting. A few more steps down, he said, 'He seems like a good boy.'

A good boy? You have no idea.

The trouble was, he *was* a good boy. Except for when he was mean. And the switch between the two was becoming more and more unpredictable. Why did he have to greet my father? Why did he have to complicate things for me?

'Can we collect the bike and go?' I asked, yanking Papa's hand.

We waited for Mummy and Neeraj to come down the steps and made our way out of the club, Papa manoeuvring the bike with both his hands. All the children hanging around in the foyer watched with envy. 'That's a boy's bike, Shweta. Are you sure you want that?' asked a boy.

I stuck my tongue out at him.

I couldn't sleep for two opposite reasons that night: the anticipation of learning to ride my treasured prize with Papa the next morning and anxiety from Angad and Papa's interaction. Why did he feel the need to suck up to Papa when he thrived on reducing me to tears?

The cycling lessons went well. My first ride was to Kanika's apartment. A few days later, Papa and Mummy received their own much-awaited prize for all their hard work: a new car. I insisted on Mummy picking me up from school, although it was only a five-minute walk from home. On a hot summer day, a gleaming, navy-blue Honda Accord, the one with enchanting headlights that opened and closed automatically, pulled up outside the school. She was an electric beauty on wheels. Even the number plate, 6668, had a nice ring to it. Although Mummy drove the car, in my mind, it was mine to show off. And showing off never felt so good. The Boys' jaws didn't close for days. I started to feel hopeful that this could be the end of it all, that they had accepted me in *their* school.

But when the novelty of the new car wore off, they started with the same old comments again. They were relentless and came very close to capsizing my already shaky confidence. In desperation, I considered sharing my deepest secret as a deflection tactic. Perhaps an exchange, a trade, would work. I was eleven-years-old and still bedwetting. An external intervention was required. But all interventions had failed thus far. I once overheard Mummy's and Papa's discussion about getting an electric blanket that emitted a small electric pulse on contact with liquid. A mild electric shock to the body. The purpose was to eventually train the mind to hold the bladder. Bedwetting was the reason I declined sleepover invites and overnight school camping trips. I hadn't even let Kanika get a whiff of this secret. It was a powerful weapon I could hand to The Boys to stop them from insulting my skin colour. I would rather be ridiculed for bedwetting. I prepared myself for the trade, such was my despondency. But what if the deflection didn't work, and they had *two* weaknesses to mock? I talked myself out of that idea quickly.

I kept that secret locked up, which was fortunate because months later one bedwetting remedy finally worked. A female doctor in India prescribed medication for three months, just one tablet before bedtime every night. It worked like magic from the first night. I eradicated this first 'B' from my life, freed myself from its bondage forever. No more added strain on Mummy for washing my bedsheets, although it hadn't sunk in yet for either of us. If it hadn't fixed itself naturally, what if it came back? What if the cure only worked for as long as the intervention did its job? Mummy was still sceptical, climbing up to the top tier of the bunk bed every morning to check my sheet herself. She continued to lay the wax cloth beneath the sheet. Finally, after a month of dry sheets, we both celebrated. The wax cloth was binned permanently, and Mummy dropped me off at Kanika's for my first sleepover. I can still remember the sensation of sleeping soundly and not waking up to a crinkling wax cloth upon every turn.

I said goodbye to the secrets and baggage I had been carrying since birth. But somehow the relief I should have felt was missing. It is said, 'A problem shared is a problem halved.' Well, this secret of mine, this problem, couldn't be shared with anyone. It's also said, 'Happiness, when shared, is doubled.' Conquering it couldn't be shared as an achievement either. The only way to feel relief was to swallow the secret. I wished I could do the same about the suspicion of being an adopted orphan. For me, sharing this was not an option either.

The year ended and I hadn't fought back the way I had planned. All that I seemingly had on my side was time. I waited patiently. We were all to move on to other pastures, to either one of the two international secondary schools in Kobe. I hoped that The Boys' presence in my life would be short-lived and that they would pick the school that I hadn't.

As much as I wished for them to pick the other school, I prayed for Kanika's parents to change their minds. Because they *did* pick the other school, despite all my attempts to convince them otherwise, on every visit. A couple of years in boarding school with one companion and a couple with another in school. And now life was catapulting me into yet another change. Aside from Kanika, I hadn't diversified my friendships, and now I was starting to realise that the repercussions would be detrimental in secondary school. I didn't have anyone to hide behind, to make the object of my affection and allow me to block out the rest of the school. Moreover, The Boys had also changed. Their pompous attitude was a portent of more abuse to come. I was about to enter a new war zone without my shield.

13

THE END

Summer of 1989, India

The summer break of 1989 didn't start well. Nana, my maternal grandfather, passed away. I was nearly twelve at the time. He had contracted diabetes a few years previously, which slowly poisoned him over many painful years.

His vision was already impaired being severely diabetic. One of his infected toes needed to be amputated the previous year. I didn't spend much time with him but cherished the time I had, sitting by him on his day bed, helping him count endless bags of coins and notes, money made from the fast-food restaurant. I remember his soothing voice, his toothless smile, his love for sweets, and his ill-discipline. It used to frustrate me how someone could indulge in food that was known to be poison for their body.

He doted on all his grandchildren and frequently rewarded us with a few coins from the stash. A classic trick every grandparent had under their sleeve, he used to ask his army of grandchildren what they preferred – one five-rupee note or three one-rupee coins. Like any other child, I used to ask for the three coins when I was younger. Despite helping him count money, I hadn't worked out that the five-rupee note held greater value, until the day I took my reward to a corner shop to buy my favourite chocolate bar.

'This is not enough money,' said the shop owner. 'You need five rupees to buy a Five Star chocolate bar.'

'You mean the note? But I have *three* coins, more than one note.'

'Another grandchild fooled,' said the shop owner, familiar with the classic trick. He laughed heartily with a mouth full of *paan* (betel leaf) and tobacco, splattering some onto his cream *kurta*.

'Numerous children come to my shop daily and return disappointed. Grandparents are very naughty, aren't they?' he remarked. 'You need five of these coins or one five-rupee note. Three coins are smaller in value than one five-rupee note. Don't tell them I told you this. And by the way, I play the same trick on my grandchildren.'

The *rupee* dropped that day. I turned around to return home with my head hanging down. Naughty grandparents indeed! From then on, I always asked my Nana for five coins. I liked the sound of the coins clanking in my hands on the way to the corner shop. Nana told me not to share the maths with the rest of the cousins. All the conversations I had ever had with him were on his day bed, now vacant. No one sat on it during the twelve days of mourning, a Hindu tradition.

There was a sombre environment in the house, but a few days into mourning, I smiled at the realisation that I would never have to see The Wicked Man again. Now that my grandfather, his friend, was gone, his visits would cease. But for now, he visited daily, at irregular times, which made it harder to avoid him. On one of those twelve days, fate brought me to him again.

Strangely, Nana's diminutive room looked even smaller now that he was gone. Although the townhouse had a main entrance, there was a side entrance through Nana's room that I preferred to use. Returning from my routine of gallivanting around the shops on the high street, I barged in to find The Wicked Man sitting on the armchair opposite the entrance. Every time I saw him, I lost my ability to think. Instead of turning around to use the main entrance, I tried walking past the armchair toward the door that led to the courtyard.

Snap. He got me, gripping my wrist again, ensuring his prey had no chance of escape.

'*Kallo*,' he said. 'Are you looking after them well?' His malicious smile suggested he had missed spewing insults at me.

Kallo. Sangeeta Mausi's nickname was passed on to me. Perhaps he missed mocking Sangeeta Mausi with that name.

'They have taken you with them so you can serve them, like a servant.'

'That's nonsense! I *am* their daughter,' I cried.

'No, you aren't. How could you even think that? *That* is utter nonsense! Didn't we already have this conversation last year? Take a glance at Chotu, the family servant. He's skinny, *kala,* and poor. Like a beggar's child. That's where you came from – a family like Chotu's.'

'That's not true!' I cried. 'That's NOT true!'

Papa heard those words, my cries. 'What's not true?' he asked, standing in the doorway. 'And why are you crying, *beta*?'

The Wicked Man let go of my wrist. I hid behind Papa

and stuttered everything he had ever said to me, for years. Papa listened in disbelief. Not that he didn't believe me. He couldn't believe that an elderly man could behave so disgracefully.

'Is this true?' he asked, glowering at The Wicked Man.

'I was only joking. I mess around with all the kids here. It doesn't mean anything,' he said, sheepishness spilling all over his words.

'It may not mean anything to you. But do you have any idea what you're doing to my child's confidence? There's a limit to joking. How dare you say to her that we left her behind in a boarding school because she doesn't belong to us, because she's dark? How dare you negate all the sacrifices we made for a better life?'

Papa turned to me, placed both his hands on my shoulders and asked, 'Is this the man who said we are ashamed of you?'

My eyes flickered, looking at The Wicked Man and then back to Papa. I nodded.

'*You* should be ashamed of yourself,' Papa told the old man. 'You couldn't find anyone but a lonely child to torture?'

This was the second time I had seen Papa raging and the first time I had witnessed his complete disregard for an elderly person. A few aunts and uncles gathered in the room, trying to pacify Papa.

'She is my child, dark or fair. It's none of your business. What good is fair skin if one is filled with darkness inside, like you? I never want to see you near her again. If I do, I will forget that you are an elderly man and apparently a friend of this family.'

Savre Mama hauled Papa out of the room. I cried harder.

Tears of joy and love for Papa gushed out. He ranted for a few more minutes then, taking a deep breath, he turned to me and said, 'Look at me, Shweta. Everything that horrible man has ever said to you is not true.'

'Papa, you said you came from a poor family. But this man says poor people are dark. Why are you fair? Mummy's fair too. And Neeraj is like you. Why am I the only one who's dark?'

'Genes are not in our hands, Shweta. You must have studied this by now in science class. Look at me, *beta*. Colour doesn't matter.'

'IT DOES TO ME! I want to be the same colour as you all!'

Papa hesitated, then said, 'Yes, you're different. *Good* different. You've got the colour of Lord Krishna.'

Coming from an atheist, a reference to Lord Krishna, one of the most worshipped gods in Hinduism, was a big deal.

'Then why do people say nasty things about colour when Lord Krishna is dark too?' I said, quizzically.

'Don't listen to people like this man. They have issues in their personal lives that manifest as bitter abuse to others.'

I nodded, wrapping my arms around him. In my heart, I knew that from this day on The Wicked Man would stay clear of me forever. He did. June 1989 was the end of my beloved Nana *and* The Wicked Man. As far as I was concerned, he was gone too. But the damage was done. I couldn't gather the courage to tell Papa that deep down inside, I had started believing the man. He was, after all, a respected friend of my Nana. Did he know something that I didn't? That I was indeed adopted? His remarks, combined with everyone else's, had almost defeated me. I had promised myself that I would fight but with how many and for how long? Wherever I went, people expressed surprise when they saw me with my family. The air hostess, Payal, Mrs Gujral, The Wicked Man, and The Boys - did all these people have issues? And who knew if there were more to come?

I had had enough of taking abuse from people who were possibly being abused themselves. I barged into Nani's room, the one with the Godrej cupboard and the files, in search of some incontrovertible proof.

'Nani, do you have my birth certificate?'

'Your *janam patri*? Yes, why do you need to see that?'

A janam patri is a star chart which notes your zodiac sign, the stars, the planets, and their positioning, based on your time of birth. That was of no use. What could the alignment of the stars and the planets have to do with proving my birth parents?

'No, Nani, my birth certificate. A piece of paper that tells you where you were born and to whom?'

'Why do you need a certificate for that, *bitiya*? I can tell you that. You were born in Kota, and I came to visit when you arrived.'

This was going nowhere. I wasn't going to be able to see what I needed to without revealing the doubt that had been inculcated in my mind.

'Never mind.'

A few nights later, I had a dream that I am still trying to erase from my memory. Papa, Mummy, Neeraj, and I were walking along a narrow, floating path that led nowhere. An endless, deep blue sea on either side, restless and ready to engulf us, sent violent waves our way. We held each other's hands and inched forward, in pursuit of a safe, steady land on the other side. The path narrowed, forcing us to walk in single file. I was the first one ahead. We inched forward with heavy, flat feet. Mummy's hand separated from mine, and the path split precisely where I stood. As I drifted further away from the rest, on a small raft, the deep blue sea turned into an ocean of lava, flames leaping high. Perhaps they were the same flames from 1984. Distraught and helpless, I stood on my raft, screaming for my family, tears evaporating from the heat within seconds. At this point in the dream, I was semi-conscious, wanting to wake up but not able to, stupefied by separation anxiety. With my eyes closed, I just watched myself disappear into the horizon of flames. This recurring dream haunted me for a few years.

I woke to find Mummy in bed next to me, fast asleep on her right arm. I placed my hand on her left forearm, controlling my panic one breath at a time.

After this nightmare, I put all my investigations to sleep forever. I wasn't going to allow anyone to come between my family and me, neither nightmares nor wicked people with issues. Fixing my one issue, my skin tone, was far less complicated than trying to understand other people's multiple issues. There were another six weeks left before the summer holiday ended, enough time for my grand plan to work.

Mummy was in the house somewhere, in one of the aunts' rooms. I went knocking on all the doors until I found her.

'Can I have five rupees for the chocolate bar? Nana used

to give it to me every day,' I said.

She reached for her thick brown wallet, bulging with rupees. When she handed me a five-rupee note, out of habit I asked for five coins and skipped my way to the corner shop.

'How much is the cream?' I said, stretching my arm, pointing to a fairness cream on the top-left shelf. I spotted the popular cream too but opted for another brand that I had seen on an aunt's dressing table.

'Who is it for?'

'My Mummy.'

'35 rupees.'

'I'll be back.' Crestfallen, I turned around to return home.

'Wait! Don't you want your chocolate?'

'Not today.'

There went my grand plan. The instructions on the tube of cream that my aunt had said fair skin can be achieved in six weeks if applied daily. I didn't have nearly enough money to buy the cream, but I was determined to see another *The End* before leaving India – the end to my colour. This cream could be my shield for secondary school. Imagining my classmates' shell-shocked faces when they laid their eyes upon my new radiant, fair complexion, I decided that however many days I had left, I would buy the cream and apply it twice a day. And this had to be done in India as I couldn't possibly pack the cream in a suitcase to take with me to Japan. Mummy packed every suitcase herself, a meticulously organised wardrobe on wheels. She could tell you exactly which suitcase of the four had an adapter, hidden under precisely seven layers of clothing on the bottom left side. A fairness cream would not go unnoticed.

I asked Mummy for the five rupees, almost daily, so that she didn't suspect anything. Carrying a bag of coins to the corner shop would be tiresome so I asked for notes instead. But where would I hide the money I had collected to purchase the cream in the first place? Under the mattress was a clichéd spot and a bad idea. Chotu picked up all the temporary bedding every morning. I couldn't hide it in the neatly organised wardrobe in the bedroom. Mummy would catch me on the first day. Stuffing the notes in my pockets was risky. If I forgot them, they would end up ruined in the laundry. The safest place to hide the money was in one of the suitcases. Mummy always unpacked the moment we set foot in our bedroom. She then put the suitcases away behind the bed and they only saw daylight again the night before we were to return to Japan.

When I finally collected enough money, I still had over four weeks to go before our return. I sprinted to the corner shop.

'Haven't seen you around in a while. Chocolate?' asked the shop owner.

'No, the cream.'

'Oh yes, for your mother.' He was a shrewd shopkeeper and remembered conversations. He used to chat with many customers, memorizing their names and their favourite purchases and even dug for gossip about their homes.

As the shopkeeper reached for the fairness cream, I cupped my hands and held them out, eagerly waiting to receive it.

'It's not like it's *prasad*,' he laughed. *Prasad* is an offering made to God and consumed as a blessing, which is what the cream felt like to me. *Prasad*. How could I disrespect it by grabbing it with one hand? This *prasad* was my portal to fairness – one simple solution to all my insecurities, enabling me to metamorphose from an ugly duckling to a beautiful swan.

Long live the fairness cream maker. How clever and thoughtful: fairness, beauty, and acceptance in a tube. They may as well have listed these on the tube.

Ingredients: *Lots of fairness, Implicit beauty, and Automatic acceptance in society*

Entranced, I daydreamed my way back home, re-igniting my aspirations of becoming a Bollywood actress. After a long time, I let my daydreams run free and unfettered, like that caramel horse at boarding school. I could ask Mummy to enrol me in dance and acting classes to hone my skills. It was all very well being one of the best dancers at the annual Diwali party in Kobe, but entertaining families at community gatherings wasn't my final destination.

Back at the house in Nani's bathroom, I squirted some cream onto my palms hastily and rubbed it all over my face. When I looked in the mirror, I was reminded of the time I had done the same with talcum powder. This looked worse. The cream hadn't spread evenly. Blotches of it made me appear ghostly white in some areas. I rubbed and rubbed but it refused to spread. Disappointed, I washed it off and hid the cream in the suitcase. In the evening, I tried again. No difference at all. I tried this for over two weeks; the cycle of rubbing and washing became increasingly frustrating. The cream didn't look or feel right on my skin.

I blamed myself; I must have not done it right. Although

I eventually tossed the cream in a mound of garbage two streets away from ours in Karol Bagh, that day marked the start of a clandestine affair with it. And with the belief that it was the one solution to eradicate all colourism-related complexes. What I hadn't realised, however, is that it was the start of a deceitful relationship – one that promised to bring a glow to my face but delivered more insecurities instead. Neither did I know that this relationship would be semi-permanent, on and off for decades.

14

NICKNAME

September 1989, Japan

The cream hadn't worked, and I was shieldless. Only one thing excited me about my new school – wearing a tie as part of the school uniform. I used to watch Papa put one on for work every morning. Ties, I thought, made you look important.

Dressed in a white shirt, grey pleated skirt, maroon and gold tie, and maroon blazer, I entered Marist Brother's International School with Mummy and Papa. Other pupils strolled in without their parents escorting them. I exchanged looks with a few of them, recognising them from the same train journey. Feeling embarrassed in the school hallway, I asked my parents to leave.

Marist, as we all called it, was a much larger school. Shaped like half a hexagon, the three arms of the building encapsulated an acre of field space with a sports hall at the far end. The school office and classrooms for 1st to 6th grade were on the ground floor. The first floor of the building was for 7th to 12th-grade classrooms. And let's not forget the toilets. A lot happened in the female toilets – girls folding their skirts up higher, exchanging school gossip, and sharing personal, intimate accounts of dates that culminated into a lot more than just a kiss.

I stepped into the 7th-grade classroom to find The Boys at the end of the room, fidgeting with their lockers. So much for hoping they would pick the other school. My stomach churned as if I was plunging down the vertical drop of a rollercoaster ride. Despite having spent three years in the previous school with them, this was the first time I *really* noticed them. Maybe because their confidence made them appear larger than the room.

Although this was their first day too, they seemed to have already settled in. New faces mixed with old, confidence mixed with nerves, apprehension mixed with excitement. The room had a strange, palpable atmosphere.

I walked to my desk, slicing through these mixed emotions, glancing at a few familiar faces from St Michael's; faces that I regretfully hadn't bothered getting familiar with when I should have. Sarina, a classmate from St Michael's, was comfortably conversing with new classmates. I always admired her confidence from afar and found her sunny disposition sometimes intimidating. Now I wished I had even a fraction of her charm. She was one whom I should have gotten to know better, but annoyingly I hadn't seized any of the previous opportunities. Here was another chance, and I wasn't going to forego it this time.

As I approached Sarina, our homeroom teacher trudged in, synchronising her timing with the school bell. Glasses resting on her head and a short bob haircut, she carried a stack of heavy textbooks and shuffled her burly body to her desk, finally relieving herself from the extra weight.

'Morning all, I am Miss Pritchett,' she greeted us. 'Your homeroom teacher this year and also your geography teacher.' Her voice projected to the back of the room, every syllable loud and clear. No welcome speech or anything of that sort. She let the voices on the school PA system handle the rest of the formalities. She reminded me of the matron at boarding school.

Miss Pritchett did a roll call, asking us for brief introductions, including any interesting facts we wanted to share about ourselves. My nerves hadn't settled yet and now this. What was I going to say in my introduction? Some revelled in talking about their favourite sport, some shared why they were attending an international school although they were Japanese. A few shared the meaning of their name. The more I thought about what I could share about myself, the more anxious I grew. A couple of classmates later, it was my turn, and I still hadn't figured out a special introduction. The meaning of my name was easy and quick.

'Shweta?' said Miss Pritchett.

'Here. My name in Sanskrit means as pure as the colour white.'

'Ha! What were your parents thinking, naming *you* that?' Angad sneered.

The room reverberated with laughter from all four corners. I joined in, laughing nervously. I missed Kanika, wishing she was there. Another friendly face, Sarina, turned from her desk to check in.

'*Blackie* is a better name for you. Suits you better,' claimed Angad a few days later.

Blackie. *Kallo*. I couldn't escape this nickname after all.

A new school, a new nickname, the same insult. He deemed me unworthy of my original name when he learned its meaning. Nicknames in Delhi and now a nickname for me here in Kobe. A few other boys joined in. Again, I had nothing better as a comeback than, 'You're a Blackie too!'

'I'm lighter than you,' Angad would say. We'd then hold out our forearms side by side to compare. I wish I had then said, 'I don't care. Colour doesn't matter to me.'

But I did care, so badly.

This nickname pierced my soul every time.

This nickname, Blackie, another 'B' in my life, trumped all other ridicules.

15

PROJECTION

August 1990, Japan

Blackie was the first word that popped into my mind upon seeing two men outside Sannomiya train station. I had been on the receiving end of this nickname for the entire school year. Today, I found myself on the giving end.

It was the first time I had visited a Japanese *onsen*, a hot spring. Visiting one was Papa's Sunday ritual, mainly because it was his relaxation time. He used to return rejuvenated and sparkling clean, as though he'd gone through a carwash.

One day, before school started again in September 1990, we insisted on going with him. He didn't seem too keen on us gate-crashing his spa party for one. But we set off to try a new *onsen* that had just opened on the other side of the mountains. Shiawase-no-Mura, The Happy Village, was a big resort, where families could spend entire weekends. What piqued my interest was travelling to the other side for the first time, setting off towards an unseen land. The exhilarating ride through a few tunnels created a sense of anticipation about discovering a mystical world. It turned out to be all the same: the same people, the same food, the same country. Even the mountains looked the same from the other side. Overall, an anti-climax, but the resort was fabulous. We all decided to make it a regular Sunday visit.

At the *onsen*, all we were given was a hand towel to cover our modesty. The hottest pool was filled with petite Japanese ladies. Heads turned when I walked in, multiple pairs of eyes examining me. Water droplets glistened on their supple, moist skin, and their cheeks blushed a rosy pink. I, on the other hand, was about to turn purple from entering the same pool. I remembered the comment from Maya Mami a few years back, that it wasn't a pretty colour on me.

Mummy shuffled her way in, avoiding any obvious puddles of water so as not to slip. No eyes scanned her, at least not the way they did me.

Grappling with being different in your own family was difficult enough. Living in Japan and being stared at also took getting used to. With dark-skinned foreigners being a rare sight, indiscreet stares were an obvious reminder of my 'alien' status in the country, like the requirement for every foreigner to register for the Alien Registration Card. That word on the card – *alien* – grated on me.

'Get in. What are you waiting for?' said Mummy, her skin already turning peachy pink. She looked like the Japanese ladies with one distinct difference – her enormous eyes.

'Why are they all looking at me?'

'Let them. It doesn't matter.'

'I don't like their stare.'

'What's gotten into you? Just get in.'

'I don't know. It's a strange kind of stare, not the friendly kind.' I hadn't even entered when a few women stood up and left the pool like they understood the conversation. I stepped in, trying to ignore the unsettling feeling.

The same happened in another tepid pool. Before I stepped in, a couple of women stared at me, then left. In the changing room, I was being stared at yet again. Frustrated, I looked back at those women and asked, 'Is something wrong?' With a high-pitched nervous giggle, they swiped their valuables and rushed out.

When we all sat down for lunch at the restaurant adjacent to the spa, I talked Papa through what had happened.

'Not many foreigners live in Kobe. They were probably staring just because they have never seen a foreigner. And this is the other side of the mountain,' he chuckled, familiar with my obsession about the other side, and slurped his ramen.

'Yes, but they didn't stare at Mummy the way they did at me,' I said. 'And why leave the pools when I enter? I felt like they left because of me.'

'You're being too sensitive. It's nothing like that.'

'It's easy for you Papa, you don't get such stares,' I sighed. 'You, Mummy, and Neeraj are foreigners too, but they don't see you as they see me – different. I deal with it every day on my school journey.' I paused. Now that I had initiated this conversation, this was the right time to bring up what I had been putting up with at school. Papa reached for his Mild Seven packet of cigarettes.

'Papa?' I said, glancing at Mummy too.

'Yes?' he said, lighting a cigarette, relaxed and all ears.

'Why did you and Mummy name me Shweta?'

'Why do you ask?'

'You said Shweta means as pure as the colour white. But I am not white!'

'You are as pure as white to us. It's not about your colour,' said both Mummy and Papa.

'It's *only* about colour at school. Angad teases me. The other boys do too. But he does a lot.'

Papa looked blankly at me, taking a drag.

'The boy who said hello to you once at The India Club when I won a bike.'

'Oh, yes. I thought you were friends.'

'Friends? Absolutely not! I hate him. He teases me for my colour.'

Say it! Tell them that he calls you Blackie. All. The. Time.

I couldn't get myself to say it. That would really upset my parents. Who knew, they might complain to the headmaster, after which my life could be a living hell.

'Angad, of all people? You tell him that beauty is only skin deep and that you care more about being beautiful in your heart. Don't stoop to his level, no matter what. He will eventually back down.'

I reflected on the advice for a nanosecond and rejected it. Calling him names was all I had! Pathetic attempts, I know, but they had started to make me feel better.

Staring out the window on the car journey back home, I pondered how to deal with the nickname and the stares. Neeraj pleaded for a McDonald's meal on the way. The closest one was opposite Sannomiya train station. It was a large station, always teeming with people who were rushing in every direction but in an orderly fashion. No one collided with one another. Outside the station were several pedestrian crossings. Mummy handed me some money, asking me to get our meals while they waited. On my walk back to the car, with a meal deal bag in either hand, I stopped. And stared.

A crowd streamed through the station doors, passengers disembarking from a packed train. Behind the crowd were two brawny and very dark African American men. Although they were quite a distance away, I picked up on their American accent. I stared, harbouring a horrible thought.

That is what 'black' skin looks like. I'm not as dark as them. Why am I called Blackie?

My stare was exactly like the one I experienced in the *onsen*. That stare made me feel utterly insignificant, yet here I was, on the other end of the same stare. I hated myself for it, knowing that I must be invoking the same emotion in those men. But I couldn't take my eyes off them. They felt the glare, like bright headlights on full beam, glared back, and looked away. I looked down, ashamed. I had wanted to fight against colour prejudice so how could I have just done what I did? I felt terrible.

Learning about Black history later that year, my eyes filled with tears the first time I saw horrific images of slavery and the suffering of Black people. Compared to what they had endured for centuries, me being called Blackie was not a big deal. Besides, I wasn't the only one with a nickname.

'Blackie, is that how much you eat?' said Ranveer in the school cafeteria, seeing my lunch plate filled with a large serving of lasagne. Ranveer, a Sikh boy, teased for his topknot in primary school, was called *Manju* – a round, Japanese mochi sweet. He eventually put his Sikhism to one side and cut his hair.

'Don't you think you should start shaving your legs, Blackie?' Nikhil said as soon as I stepped into the classroom. Nikhil, still a babyface at 12, was called *Akachan* – Baby.

'Blackie can't shoot!' said Manish, watching the girls' team play soccer after school. Jiro, one of our Japanese classmates, nicknamed Manish, *Chibi* (Shorty), until he outgrew him. The Boys also called him Monkey when he was part of their gang.

'We can't see you, Blackie,' said Angad in the AV room when the lights were turned off for movies. Angad's nickname was Goggle-Eyed, given to him by none other than The Boys. I would call him that too.

An overweight Japanese girl, Yuki was nicknamed *Buta* – pig. Faiza, called Beaver, was ridiculed for her teeth. *Dorobo* – meaning burglar – was Rahul's nickname, owing to his premature stubble, giving him a rough look.

I wanted to speak out against all the name-calling. I should have done so. But once again, I weaselled out, letting everyone fight their own battles. After all, I was fighting mine all alone. On second thought, I weaselled out of fighting mine too.

Blackie was just one nickname among all the others. My classmates didn't seem that affected by their names. Perhaps they were better at putting on a poker face. Or perhaps mine affected me more because it triggered my deepest fear about possibly being adopted, of being different to the family. How could I outgrow my colour, anyway?

Putting on a brave face was the only option at the time.

It's just a nickname. It doesn't mean anything.

16

FRENEMY

October 1990, Japan

'Let's perform with the boys this year for the Diwali ball,' Sarina suggested.

Stupid idea. It will get vetoed immediately, by all.

It didn't. Both the boys and the girls were up for it.

The arrival of October meant preparations were in full swing for the annual grand Diwali ball. The Indian community in Kobe was so small, there were barely enough families to call it a community. Everyone knew everyone, and everyone socialised with everyone, every weekend. There was only one way to become an integral part of this group – by becoming a member of The India Club. Attending the Diwali ball was a cultural protocol. If you chose not to attend, people would interrogate you the next day, wanting valid reasons for your absence.

Every year, there was fierce competition among children and young adults to choose the latest Bollywood song for their performance. We had to reserve the song on the club's performance list before anyone else did. The latest trend was for the boys and girls to perform together, dancing hand-in-hand to romantic Bollywood songs, notwithstanding the relationship they had in real life.

The Girls – Sarina, Faiza, and I – had started spending more time with The Boys – Nikhil, Angad, Manish, and Ranveer – much to my disapproval. More girls and boys from the year below us would often join us. Some crushes and romantic relationships had begun to bloom. Between Angad and me, there was only room for one emotion: hatred. Yet The Boys and The Girls started socialising on Saturday nights more and more frequently. I was expected to be friendly with a brown boy who hadn't stopped calling me Blackie. Angad became my 'frenemy', adding yet another layer of confusion.

One Saturday night, we all met up outside The India Club and dawdled down towards Sannomiya station to an Italian restaurant. As early as 7 p.m., some tipsy Japanese men staggered along the streets with bright red faces, after only a couple of drinks. Papa used to say the Japanese have a low tolerance for alcohol.

'*Anatano mei oki ne, kirei ne*. Your eyes are big and beautiful,' some of them said. I had heard Mummy receive this compliment many times. I liked it when I received it today. During my time in Japan, I received this compliment countless times. It seemed like the Japanese wanted my eyes. I wanted their colour. But the eyes of drunk men on me reminded me of an uncle, The Creepy Man, in my paternal grandparents' home. Whenever I saw him, he had a drink in his hand. And whenever I felt his bulging eyes on me, his sinister stare left me feeling unsettled in a way I didn't understand then. Unlike The Wicked Man, this uncle never said anything. His eyes used to follow me until I was out of his sight, malevolent intentions written all over them. Incomprehensible but creepy. I remember my inner voice telling me I needed to avoid him at any cost, even more than The Wicked Man.

I shied away from the men, sandwiching myself between the others. The closer we got to Sannomiya station, the busier the streets, bustling with family-owned ramen shops. Bright lights of pharmacies, cosmetic shops, and Lawson convenience stores spilt onto the pavements. Every time someone entered a store or a restaurant, '*Irasshaimase*, Welcome,' echoed outside. The muffled sound of poorly attempted singing to Michael Jackson or Madonna songs in karaoke parlours was both cringy and endearing. Many young teenagers, boys and girls, roamed around with blond streaks in their hair and blue contact lenses. Two quaint Shinto shrines had freshly lit incense sticks. The aroma of grilled chicken, garnished with a generous drizzle of teriyaki sauce, sizzling on hot iron, was making me hungry.

'That chicken smells delicious,' I said, turning my nose toward a little restaurant.

'You eat meat?' Angad asked, his eyebrows raised.

'Yes, you have a problem with that too?' As soon as the words left my mouth, I feared the consequences. I often snapped at him and allowed him an easy victory.

Our peacemaker, Sarina, put out the fire before it spread, before we burned each other with our animosity. Things had become complicated for Sarina and me. Her parents and Angad's parents were close friends, the two of them having a sibling-like relationship. Therefore, she often restrained herself from intervening when Angad and I were locked in yet another altercation.

I was facing Sheetal and Payal all over again. Sheetal too would often use deflection to get Payal off my back.

'Let's pick a song now,' Sarina said.

'How about *Dum Duma Dum* from the movie *Dil*?' I said.

Damn it! Could you not keep your mouth shut? Why did you have to suggest a song?

A few other suggestions were made, but we all agreed on *Dum Duma Dum*, a battle of the sexes song. We also agreed that I would choreograph it. At the restaurant, we waited in the queue for nearly an hour. It didn't occur to any of us insouciant teenagers to reserve a table for ten.

After all of us ordered variations of the same dish, pizza, and Coke, the evening transpired to be a memorable one, full of cackles, some leg-pulling, and lots of gossip. The boys were entertaining, especially the repartee between them.

We exchanged notes on the latest episode of *Beverly Hills 90210* and lamented about a Japanese TV series, which I didn't watch, coming to an end. Because Papa encouraged me to take French lessons in school instead of Japanese, my Japanese never improved beyond a conversational level. A couple of years later, French lessons were a complete write-off too since I couldn't practise the language in Japan. I discreetly switched the conversation from the Japanese TV series to crushes on teachers, an evergreen hot topic among teenagers. The temperature on our table rose along with the noise level. We received disapproving glares from every other table. Our waiter came over twice, asking us to keep it down. Another subject change was the only way to curb our excitement.

'So, you eat chicken, Shweta?' asked Angad again.

I couldn't believe what I had just heard. *Did he call me Shweta? Not Blackie? Play it cool.*

'Yeah, so?'

'Aren't you meant to be vegetarian? You're a Hindu, right?'

'Yes . . . so?'

'You choose to eat meat when you shouldn't.'

'Yes, I like it.'

'You like eating an animal?'

'Stop it, will you?!' Nikhil pleaded. 'You argue like a married couple!'

'Married? Over my dead body,' Angad and I said simultaneously, shuddering in disgust.

Angad didn't call me Blackie all evening. That bothered me.

If you're going to call me Shweta, the least I expect is an apology and a song and dance.

I hated being called Blackie but had gotten used to it. Just as the others had. No one else noticed the switch. It was a change I should have welcomed with open arms. Did that mean we were friends now? If his attention had shifted to my non-vegetarianism, I was more than happy to argue over the matter for eternity.

On the way home, more tipsy men faltered on the streets. Pachinko parlours, gambling arcades full of low-stakes slot machines, were heaving with almost every seat occupied.

The pavements were even busier as though everyone was out for a street party. I started thinking ahead of possible names Angad might call me from tomorrow. Chicken Eater, Chicken Killer, Traitor Hindu - I didn't mind any of them so long as Blackie was finally out.

Before we all said goodbye, we had agreed to meet up again on Sunday morning at The India Club to reserve our song and begin our first rehearsal. I danced home, excited to plan the choreography.

Mummy and Papa were having their own share of Saturday night fun, playing Rummy with friends, including Mrs Gujral. I hated having to be courteous to her, to greet her, but I did. I scanned the room, said a quick hello to everyone, and settled down opposite the TV. Playing the movie on mute, I had only just started emulating the dance moves when my focus was disrupted by a commotion of raised voices asking Mummy to reveal her cards.

'Veena, we know you picked up two cards from the stack,' said Mr Sharma.

'I didn't,' chuckled Mummy. 'See, just one card.' She flashed one card to everyone.

'We all saw it. You know you did,' said everyone around the table.

'Madam Ji, did you pick up another card?' asked Papa. His term of endearment for her, *Madam Ji*, still rings in my ears sometimes.

'No, I'm telling you I didn't.'

'Well, if she's saying she didn't, then she didn't,' Papa insisted.

But Mummy's silent laugh gave it away. She used to

deliberately cheat, knowing she had the worst poker face. Her laughter, which began with sound and quietened to silent vibrations was the sweetest thing about her. She would cheat out of boredom, to break up the sobriety in the room. When the four of us played cards on Sunday afternoons, Mummy would do the same, and we all loved her for it. 'I grew up with seven siblings. If you didn't cheat, you never had a chance of winning,' she would chuckle.

Papa knew every little habit of Mummy's and vice versa. They never ganged up on each other as far as others were concerned. Their little quarrels never developed into serious arguments, apart from the time when Neeraj went missing.

'OK, Madam Ji, let's drop it,' Papa would say.

Married couples. This was what married couples were like to me. Nothing but love, understanding and standing up for each other. 'You argue like a married couple' were Nikhil's words earlier. Our science teacher in school had said the same one day in class, observing our daily bickering. I didn't think married couples argued. How could Nikhil make such a comment about Angad and me?

The next morning, I was the first to arrive, waiting on the stage of the club. I had practiced enough dance steps for one day's rehearsal, tested the cassette, and set it to exactly where the song started. Everything was set except the pairings.

'You two should pair up together,' said one of The Boys to Angad and me.

'Ha, no chance. I don't want to be paired with Blackie,' said Angad.

The trouble with a frenemy is that you always give them the benefit of the doubt, hoping they will treat you as a friend. Then they turn up with their enemy hat on instead. Yesterday I was Shweta. Today I was Blackie.

After what seemed like hours of discussion, everyone concluded that we should pair up together.

'Stop arguing, you two. Can you not do what works best for the group? And what are you complaining about?' said Sarina, turning to Angad. 'For being paired up with the best dancer, who will make you look good?'

Angad conceded. So did I because I didn't want to be a nuisance for the group and was desperate to perform. Dancing for Diwali held the same excitement as the countdown to Christmas.

Besides, Blackie didn't hurt as much anymore. Like everything else, I sucked up this capital B, bracing myself for the masochistic ride ahead with a frenemy.

17

THE LION AND THE HARE

December 1990, Japan

It was during a Christmas school assembly when Angad struck. . .just like The Wicked Man. Perhaps he felt the need to after having had to dance with me. Perhaps I was wrong in deducing that performing together would change our relationship. Perhaps he didn't realise how much he was about to overstep the mark.

Seventh-grade students had been seated in the cafeteria, which also doubled up as a school hall. When our class, the eighth grade, was called up to take our seats, the boys were ahead of the girls. They took their seats, filling the hall from back to front, followed by the girls in front of them. Angad sat diagonally behind my right shoulder. The Christmas assembly was about to start, with children from the Reception class presenting their play as the opening act. But they were delayed because one child's nerves got the better of him. Chattering filled the room in anticipation, and the teachers didn't bother hushing us.

'Hey, Blackie,' Angad said, prodding my shoulder with one finger. I ignored him. 'Your little brother will be performing today, right? I've seen him. He's fair too. Why is your colour different from your family's? Don't you want to know why? Don't you ever ask your parents?'

My anger was simmering but I continued to ignore him, taking deeper breaths. Perhaps he observed my chest movement in his peripheral vision. Or perhaps my shoulders gave it away, moving up and down more noticeably. He prodded my shoulder again.

'Do your parents have your birth certificate? I bet they don't. Or they are hiding it from you because the only explanation for the difference is that you don't belong to them. You must be adopted.'

The same words as The Wicked Man. Adopted.

'Shut up, Angad!' I snapped, turning to him. I saw The Wicked Man in him.

'How do you know you're not adopted?'

'Because I know, OK? Everyone says I look like my mother.'

'Exactly. Maybe they are only half your parents.'

'What the hell are you getting at?'

'Your mother is your mother but your father . . .'

'Don't even think about finishing that sentence, you asshole!'

The lava bubbling inside of me was out. I thought I had more, but any further words sat on the tip of my tongue and refused to cooperate.

'Shut up, Angad! Know when to stop!' Sarina barked from beside me. She usually refrained from getting involved in our feuds.

He really didn't know when to stop. 'You know what it means to be a bastard?'

The final eruption was internal, savagely incinerating no one else but me. This was the day Angad crossed the line. For the five years that I had endured the insults, I had not imagined his obnoxious temerity, fuelled by my stoic silence, would result in him attacking my mother. I was now being labelled with yet another capital 'B' – this time a Bastard. I wasn't going to allow nicknames to define me any longer.

Bedwetter

Beggar's Child

Black Sheep

Bad apple

Blackie

Bastard

I don't remember any of the assembly's acts after that, not even my brother's performance. From that day, retribution consumed me. I felt a massive surge of confidence, and I liked it. No longer was I prepared to dodge any remarks, stay quiet, or hide behind my parents, expecting them to report bullying to the school. This battle was solely mine and losing was not an option. There was going to be only one outcome. Angad had to be silenced once and for all; he had to be taught a lesson.

My favourite bedtime story, a tale about reflection, kept creeping into my mind. I vividly remember Papa's narration.

Once upon a time, there lived a ferocious lion in a jungle. He killed any animal that came his way. The jungle's animal kingdom began to shrink fast. Worried, all the animals congregated and went to meet the lion.

'O king of the jungle,' said all the animals. 'We have a small request.'

'Go on,' said the lion, uninterested.

'You are the king of the jungle. However, there won't be many animals left to rule if unnecessary killings carry on,' said the animals.

This caught the lion's attention; he didn't want to lose his reign over the animals.

'We propose to send you one animal a day for your food,' said the animals.

The lion agreed and from that day on, all the animals drew names to pick the lion's prey for the day.

One day, it was the hare's turn. All the animals said their goodbyes to the hare and sent him off. The hare, a clever animal, was not prepared to die this way. When he came across a deep well on the way, he wove a plan. He slept by the well and made his way to the lion a few hours later.

The hare saw the lion pacing back and forth, hungry and furious.

'How dare you come so late?' said the lion, raging. 'And you, a tiny hare, are my meal today?'

'Forgive me, O mighty lion,' said the hare. 'I was on my way to you but another lion in the jungle stopped me. He wanted me for his meal.'

'What?! Another lion in my jungle?' The lion commanded the hare to take him to the other lion immediately.

The hare led the lion to the well. 'The other lion is in there,' he said, stepping back from the well. The lion edged closer to the well and peeped in. Inside the well, he could see another lion looking up at him. The lion roared in anger. The roar echoed back. The lion thought it was the other lion challenging him. The lion jumped in, ready to fight the other lion. But what he did not realise was that he had merely seen his own reflection, heard his own roar.

That day was the end of the wicked lion.

How could I show Angad *his* reflection? Unlike the lion, Angad had me, and just me, as a meal every day. For every day that he called me Blackie, he ravaged a little piece of me, chewing away at my self-confidence. I had to find a way to be the brave hare.

I maintained my silence for the last couple of school days. Then, during the Christmas break, I confided in Kanika. We had drifted apart over the years but had recently rekindled our friendship. She emboldened me to stand up to Angad.

'Let's get him when he least expects it,' she said. 'Don't react for a few months. It will be hard but remain silent. Let him believe he's got you.'

'I can't. He implied that I am a bastard!'

'You have to. And it will be worth it.'

I huffed and agreed reluctantly.

'What shall I say to him? Or do?'

'Saying anything won't achieve what you want, which is to shut him up for good.'

What she suggested next stunned me. Inspired by *The Lion and the Hare* story, I hadn't told her that I was thinking of acquainting him with his true self. Although we had parted ways for a couple of years, my bond with Kanika was still strong; we could telepathically read each other's thoughts.

'You need to make him see who he *really* is.'

'That's exactly what I had in mind. How, though? Wait, I've got it! I should put a mirror in his locker with a note.'

'That won't cut it,' she laughed. 'He probably looks into a mirror every day but doesn't see his true self.'

'OK. What, then?'

Kanika said she could get me something that Angad would remember for life. 'Wait to give it to him on a special occasion, like his birthday.'

'That's months away. I can't wait that long.'

The next special occasion was on 14 February 1991, Valentine's Day. Until then, I had the same nightmare a few times, the one where I drifted away from my family on a raft surrounded by violent waves or flames. Occasionally, it was a sea of black tar. I would wake up sweating, get dressed for school, and pretend that things were all good between Angad and me, counting down to Valentine's Day.

Ten minutes before our lunch break ended, before everyone returned to the classroom, I unzipped my school bag and pulled out a small gift box, about the size that would contain a watch. Angad's locker had been left open. The determination that came over me that moment held my hands steady. In the past, my heart used to pound for simply calling him a name back.

I placed the gift box and a note in his locker, right on the edge so he couldn't miss it. Then, I walked back to my desk, sat, and waited. He entered the classroom a few minutes before the bell rang. Ideally, I was hoping the entire class would be present when he opened the box, but only a handful of classmates were back.

'Ah, looks like I have a secret admirer,' Angad gloated upon opening his locker. He wore the biggest grin I had ever seen on him. I quickly turned around, facing the other way, pretending to be preoccupied with homework. He walked with the gift to his desk.

'Who could this Valentine's gift be from?' His voice was rising as he narrated the experience to the class. It worked. Some classmates turned towards him, eager to find out what was in the box. As he ripped every layer of wrapping paper (there were several of them), my heart was racing with anticipation. For once, I was crystal clear about my actions. Come what may, I was prepared to fight and there was no turning back. The fear of detention, of the complaint reaching my parents, didn't weaken my valour.

He dramatized the act; I wanted to get up and open the box for him myself. But his narration was entertaining. The more he gloated, the more intense his shock would be, and the more fulfilling my revenge.

Then he went quiet. It was a moment of pure joy, or pride, rather. I turned to see his face, numb with shock, staring at his present.

'What is it, Angad? Why do you look shocked?' asked one classmate.

Angad didn't utter a word. He looked directly at me, knowing I was responsible for the gift. I laughed uncontrollably, swelling with satisfaction.

'What does the note say, Angad?' someone asked again.

I saw Angad's eyes trace the words.

This is who you are, and this is your colour.

Realising that I had given the gift, everyone gathered around Angad's desk, desperate to see it.

'Really, Shweta?' said Angad.

'Yes really, Angad. I hope you see yourself in that,' I said, exulting over my victory.

At last, Angad saw his reflection and more importantly, my fearless self. Others in the classroom, having seen the gift, joined me in the laughter. Some thought the gift was harsh, saying, 'Shweta, don't you think this is a bit much? Aren't you overreacting?'

Years of demeaning words, because they were intangible, had gone unnoticed. Yet this one tangible gift was seen as harsh. Perhaps it was. Perhaps Angad had borne the brunt of my pain unfairly. But in my eyes, only Angad deserved it because he had questioned my belonging. Angad, a brown boy himself.

'Not at all. I have let him off easily.' I smiled, holding my head up high.

His present was a piece of fake, plastic poop. Call it showing him his reflection or giving him a dose of his own medicine. I did my best to refrain from such tactics. However, this was the one time when it was the only resort. In my younger years, when my parents used to recite the story of *The Lion and the Hare* to me, they told me I would always clap at the end, pleased to hear the lion reach his deserved destiny. But I never applauded the hare for his prowess, without which all the forest animals would have been devoured. That Valentine's Day, I clapped for the hare *and* for myself. I had no regrets. Could I have come up with something classier as a lesson, at the age of thirteen? Possibly. Did it work? Absolutely.

Valentine's Day 1991 was the last time Angad and the rest of The Boys called me Blackie. Angad never asked for a specific reason for the gift. And I never told him. Sometimes, I wondered if he even understood what *bastard* really meant. Was it just a word that sounded funny to him? The acrimonious relationship between us took a while to bloom into an amicable one. But once it did, there were no blurred lines, no guessing games, and no colour-related taunts, at least not in Kobe. The summer breaks in India, however, still had plenty in store.

18

A NARROW ESCAPE

Summer 1991, India

Baba, my paternal grandfather, made heads turn; he was that handsome, even in his sixties. A prominent mole on his left cheek aside, small, light-brown eyes and a sharp nose gave him an intriguing edge. He had locks of black and grey hair and was even fairer than Papa.

Every summer holiday, he would stay up, no matter how late, waiting for us to arrive home from the airport. Then, upon seeing us, he would grant us a faint smile. That was as far as he would go to display his affection. He didn't interact much with his grandchildren, especially his granddaughters. Sometimes, I could tell that he wanted to, seeing him join a conversation and smile from a distance. If he entered the room, my aunts would stand up and cover their heads with their saris. Although I never said anything, I disapproved of the degree of his patriarchal status. Despite that, we had a peculiar bond, limited to mid-afternoon foot massages. He told me I had a soft touch and would cajole me into giving him a massage almost every day during the summer holidays. I didn't mind because I was rewarded with five rupees.

Only a week into the summer holiday, however, this bonding time came to an end when I faced his wrath one afternoon.

'Where have you been?' he yelled, reaching for my left ear, twisting it hard. Like the teacher in the boarding school did before she slammed the ruler on my knuckles.

'Only across to the neighbours,' I cried, folding my arms behind my back. I had made good friends with two teenagers in our neighbouring family, a boy and a girl. The boy and I were the same age. But I wasn't interested in him; it was his sister whose company I enjoyed. I was at their house playing Uno and had asked for Mummy's permission before I went. When I came back an hour later, Baba opened the door.

Holding on to my left ear, he dragged me to his room while I tried to figure out what I had done wrong and the reason for his vagarious outburst.

'You will never go again. Do you understand? Never!'

'But why?'

'Don't ask any questions! Do as you are told.'

'But what's wrong with going to play? You've never objected to any of us going to play with them before today.'

Mummy heard the commotion and scurried in, but to no avail. Baba still hadn't let go of my ear.

'She asked me if she could go,' said Mummy in a submissive tone, covering her head with her sari.

'Your daughter is coming of age. Don't you think she should not be mingling with boys anymore? Who knows what the kids could get up to?'

'Baba, please let go.' My ear was throbbing with pain.

'I won't go again.'

He lowered his head, staring at me. I could see he was expecting more.

'I'm sorry, Baba,' I apologised.

As soon as he let go, I ran up the stairs to our bedroom. I didn't understand what he meant by 'coming of age'. What could happen? Mummy then explained that once a girl starts her period, she transitions from childhood to womanhood, after which stricter rules apply for playing with boys.

'He means well. He's just trying to protect you,' she mollified.

'Protect me by hurting me? And from what?' I asked, rubbing my ear.

'Your body shape is changing. As a woman, you start to become more attractive to boys.'

I wish! How I wished that if my body was changing, there was some way to change my colour too. None of the boys in school were attracted to me. At school discos, no boy ever asked me to join him for a slow dance.

'I attend a co-ed school and hang out with boys every day.'

'Things in Japan are different. Here, we must abide by the rules of your grandparents.'

I didn't visit the neighbours again. Nor did I visit Baba's room. He never yelled at me again, but I did not trust his capriciousness. I was not prepared to be punished harshly in case he was having a bad day. Every time he called me to massage his feet, I ran the other way.

A few weeks later, the family was hosting prayers over multiple days at a nearby temple hall. Men sat on the left and women on the right, a narrow passage splitting the two groups. This was the day The Creepy Man spoke to me directly for the first time, and I understood why his stares gave me the shivers.

By sheer coincidence, my first period announced my entry into womanhood days after Baba's outburst. And overnight, my hormones instructed my brain: grow up. Suddenly, I became very aware of the sensation of attraction. I understood the double meaning behind some of the scenes in Bollywood movies, although I would pretend in front of my parents that I hadn't a clue. I also began to understand the difference between good attraction and bad attraction. Scenes about marriage consummation were very common in Bollywood films in the '90s, but so were *izzat looting* (rape) scenes. The two were a standard formula, as though such scenes would guarantee a hit. Some rape scenes were almost glorified, going as far as blaming the victim for dressing provocatively. All the villains portrayed in the movies had an uncanny resemblance to The Creepy Man. And all I wanted was to never see him again.

That afternoon, the temple hall was filled with our family, extended family, and the wider community. On such occasions, it was impossible to do a headcount to identify missing members, if at all. I wish I had known who was missing. I could feel my second period coming. As it was forbidden for a woman to be in a place of worship during her menstrual cycle, I had to leave immediately. Getting my period in India was not a pleasant experience in any sense. It was enraging. Though I was taught in school that a girl starting her period is a sign of fertility, giving herself and others the joy of being able to bear a child, my two grandmothers treated me like an Untouchable for three days.

'Don't come close,' they said, stepping further away. 'And don't enter the kitchen. You must sit away from the rest of the family when eating. And when you're done, you must wash your dishes and leave them outside the kitchen, lathered in soap. One of your aunts will pick it up. And you must wash your hair on the third day.'

'What happens on the third day? My period lasts for at least five days. Why am I considered *clean* on the third day?'

'It's the tradition.'

Mummy was my only means of getting answers that made sense because I hadn't seen her abide by this tradition in Kobe. 'Of course, I can't observe this in Kobe. I am the only woman in the house, looking after the family. How would I run the house if I sat out of the kitchen for three days?'

'So…you're *allowed* to bend the rules?'

'Yes, because I have no choice.'

'Getting your period isn't a choice either! How can women treat other women like this?'

'It's not the women. These are the customs of our society.'

'Who created these customs?'

'I don't know. The gatekeepers of our religion, I suppose.'

'You mean men? What do men know about periods? And unless these gatekeepers were dropped from heaven, I'm guessing women gave birth to them?'

Mummy's patience, a flickering candle, was about to extinguish at any moment. She had only one response to my rebellious interrogation: 'Such are the ways here. Do it while you're in India.'

With every trip to India, she had started to resort to that line. I was quickly gaining a reputation as the feisty, outspoken one. This was not well received by the older members of the family. Questioning almost every belief was partly down to projection – if I couldn't openly speak about colourism due to my cowardice, I was certainly going to overcompensate and challenge all other impractical notions. Puberty hormones were partly to blame. Anything, and I mean *anything*, the family said had to be challenged without vaguely processing what was said.

On my short walk back home from the temple, I realised I was going to be treated like an Untouchable for three days. When I reached home, I found all the rooms had been locked. The only one that was open (and the only room that provided access to our family bedroom upstairs) was occupied by The Creepy Man. And two other men. All three were engaged in alcoholic debauchery, drinking mid-afternoon. They appeared to have had a few. A bottle of Johnny Walker whisky sat on the central coffee table, their glasses half-filled with the golden drink. Papa used to have the same drink occasionally.

They watched me walk warily through the narrow passage between the couches and the coffee table towards the door that led to the staircase. I jittered inwardly, trying to appear nonchalant to their lecherous glares. Avoiding any eye contact, I focused on my brown, strappy sandals, clutched my red ankle-length skirt, and kept walking. As I did, I happened to glance at the television simply because it was on. All three of them were engrossed in the sight of a radiant, fair-skinned woman, draped in a white sari, bathing under a waterfall. The drenched sari highlighted every contour of her body. The camera zoomed in on the shape of her ample breasts, then her waist, then her legs. Water trickled down her shoulders, bare arms, and waist; her skin glistened like sun rays on the surface of the oceans.

Embarrassed, I blushed. The Creepy Man was sitting on the armchair closest to the door, about to take a sip of his drink, light bouncing off his completely bald head. He was skinny like a scarecrow with a huge pot belly poking out of his faded white shirt.

When I approached the door, he said, 'Shweta, tell me…' I caught his eyes gradually travelling down to my chest. 'Do you bathe like her too?'

The predatory smile that escaped his moustache-covered lips paralysed me. I froze on the spot. My stomach churned with his lascivious gaze. I recognised that look from numerous previous interactions. Today, I understood what that look meant: dirty, hideous intentions.

'No,' I said, my voice drowned by the ceiling fan, spinning at full speed. At that moment, I felt as if I could hear every blade completing a full circle. I wondered which direction the fan would take if by freak accident it flew out of its socket. Mummy's words - 'You become more attractive as your body changes' - echoed in my head. I had wanted to feel attractive for so long, but on that day, I wished the opposite.

I didn't *want* to say anything, but I don't know what possessed me to speak, as if this inappropriate question from an uncle to a teenage niece was a normal conversation. Perhaps I wanted to give him the impression that it didn't bother me. If I reacted adversely, it might have spurred him on as he sensed my fear. I wanted to turn around and run out of the room and back to the temple. But the other two men were closer to the exit door. My only escape route was through the door next to The Creepy Man.

Move, damn it! Move!

Somehow, I mustered the courage to walk out of the door and up the stairs. All the rooms upstairs were locked, except a small pantry, a bathroom, and our bedroom. I hurried into our bedroom and double-locked the door.

Debilitating cramps hindered my ability to consider how I would protect myself should the worst happen. I didn't want to take any chances and come out of the room for a glass of water from the pantry. Instead, I rummaged through the wardrobe for a medicine kit. If I found it, I was prepared to chew the bitter pain relief tablets. But I found nothing.

I sat on the super-king-sized bed, praying for someone to return from the temple. With my eyes fixated on the door and my ears perked up to detect the slightest of sounds, I rocked back and forth on the bed. The room was a furnace as I hadn't turned on the noisy air conditioner; it was imperative that I hear any movement.

Why me?

I shuffled to the middle of the bed, to align myself with the full-length mirror on the wooden wardrobe opposite the bed. I didn't see anything worth lusting over. In fact, I didn't see anything special at all, not that day or any day previously. When anyone paid me a compliment, I didn't know how to accept it graciously. I didn't believe in the authenticity of any praise relating to my physical appearance. How could someone less than ordinary looking, whose self-esteem was buried deeper than an ocean trench, be attractive to anyone?

There were much more attractive cousins and aunts in the family. Fair, beautiful, and womanlier.

This uncle didn't just happen to say something stupid at that moment. He hadn't behaved like a good uncle before this. He had made me uncomfortable for almost two years. Why did he have eyes for me?

As much as I tried to convince myself that what happened downstairs wasn't a big deal, my mind kept pointing to these factors:

Three intoxicated men

A seductive scene on television

One perverted uncle

One kinky comment

No one in the house

All other rooms locked

One helpless teenager

And that they all led to one very strong possibility. I couldn't get myself to even think it. Three men easily had the combined strength to knock a door down. If they did, I had no escape route. Perhaps I had misconstrued the scenario in my mind. Could delirium from the pain have exaggerated it all? Or perhaps I was right to panic.

Close to fainting from panic and pain, I was shaken by the sound of heavy footsteps dragging up the stairs. The thoughts that went through my mind were too gruesome to complete themselves. The footsteps were of a single person. With every step inching closer to the bedroom, my body felt heavier, incapable of moving. I couldn't think of anywhere to hide apart from the most obvious – under the bed, just as I had during the riots in 1984. I remembered those flames.

I would have rather been burnt alive then. I shut my eyes, muttering, 'Mummy, please come back.' And then I held my breath, wanting to remain dead silent.

The footsteps paused. Then they tottered down.

I gasped to catch my breath. After the longest 45 minutes of my life, I heard footsteps up the stairs again. By this time, I didn't have any energy left to react. There was no fear, no pain, just numbness. There was a loud, abrupt banging on the door. The banging paused for a second, then got louder and more aggressive.

'Shweta? Are you in there?'

It was Mummy! The relief. It was as if I had been drowning and finally drawn up to catch a breath. I jumped out of the bed to open the door, my top drenched in sweat.

'What's the matter? Why do you look like you've seen a ghost?'

'My...I have bad cramps. I couldn't find the medicine kit and have been waiting for you.'

'Why are you shivering? It's almost 40 degrees outside and even hotter in the room.' She touched my forehead.

'I'm fine. Please find the tablets. I can't bear the pain.'

'It's right here in the wardrobe.' She lifted a few layers of clothes, unzipped a black pouch, and handed me two tablets.

As I popped the tablets, I heard more family members downstairs. Everyone was back. I jumped back on the bed and fell asleep within moments.

When I woke up, the cramps had subsided, and I contemplated telling Mummy what had happened. There was no point. The uncle would deny it, and the awkwardness within the family would be so great, the only resolution would be to disown him or disown me. This just meant disowning me because it was easier to disown a rebellious – and possibly adopted – female teenager than an uncle. I *would* be The Black Rose.

From that day, I avoided The Creepy Man at all costs. I showered only when he was not present in the house. I didn't want to risk running into him with a towel in my hand, entering or exiting the bathroom with wet hair. I wanted to strip his imagination, not permitting any dirty thoughts to develop. During every shower, my eyes would be glued to the narrow slit at the bottom of the door, looking for visible signs of anyone lurking close to the door.

I would walk past him, greet everyone in a room full of family members except him. In a large family, everyone was too busy to notice this snub. He tried to talk to me a few times, asking me to bring ice for his drink or to inform an aunt to lay the table for dinner. I ignored him. He never complained to anyone either. If he did, he knew he was at risk of revealing his dirty self.

Three days later, I was 'allowed' back at the temple. When I saw Baba sitting cross-legged in the front row, I muttered under my breath from afar, 'You put a restraining order on me for seeing a harmless thirteen-year-old boy. In your eyes, to protect me. Can you protect me from men in the family who could be capable of much worse than you could ever imagine?' These words never came out loud. I buried this secret too.

At first, I couldn't see The Creepy Man sitting among all the men. I sighed with relief, a little too soon. He stood, palms pressed together, opposite one of the deity statues, Goddess Durga. He must have known I was watching him. He turned slightly, aiming his ugly smile at me. I continued to stare at him.

With all the dirty intentions you harbour about the female form, you have the audacity to pray to a goddess?

When he left, I walked around the temple in amazement, counting the various goddesses. There was one statue that differed from the rest, the only one made from black marble. Goddess Kali. *Goddess Black*, I translated in my head.

19

DARKNESS

The same day

I stood gazing at Goddess Kali's statue, trying to untangle my pride and anger. I couldn't work out if I should feel elated or deflated. Here I was, face to face with a goddess who could be an ambassador for all dark-skinned females. Or was Her black colour validation of colourism and proof that it existed in the heavenly world too? Why were all other goddess statues made of white marble?

I grabbed the attention of a heavy-set priest waddling past. 'Why is She black?' I asked. Upon taking a closer look, I noticed Her red, lolling tongue, ten arms – one of which carried the decapitated head of a demon – and a garland of skulls.

'She's a reincarnation of Goddess Durga, who took the form of Kali to slay demons,' the priest replied. To me, *Her* appearance was demonised, and I couldn't make any sense of it. Frankly, I wasn't interested in the other details of Her appearance. It was Her colour that drew me.

'Yes, but why did She have to be *kali*? Why couldn't She be like the other goddesses?'

'Because She's a slayer. A goddess whose wrath transforms Her into this form. She comes from the depths of darkness, from death.'

'I understand what She does, but that doesn't answer my question. I'm asking about Her colour. Why does She have to be black? She can come from darkness, but She doesn't need to be dark Herself. She's a goddess who slays demons, which is why we pray to Her, so why is She depicted in black?'

He huffed, shook his head and left me with more questions.

A week later, when Mummy asked me if I wanted to go to Vaishno Devi, a pilgrimage to Goddess Durga's temple, I immediately said yes. I had heard that millions of men and women visited Vaishno Devi in Jammu, a beautiful mountainous state, every year and I needed to understand why. If Kali is an avatar of Goddess Durga, surely some priest at her holy temple was bound to have answers.

I started the same conversation with a priest there; I received the same answers, as though the priests had read the same book but only halfway. They didn't have answers.

Mummy, seeing the priest's agitation, nudged me to keep walking. Getting no answers from two men of religious authority only released a flood of extra questions in my mind, but they were held back by the crowds of visitors at the temple.

'She comes from darkness, from death' were the priests' words. Yet She was worshipped. She was depicted with skin as black as a moonless night, yet millions paid their respects to Her. I wondered how many also passed judgement on dark-skinned people, how many men demanded fair wives, how many women struggled to become suitably fair, all the while queuing up for one glimpse of Goddess Kali at their local temple, idolising Her.

I felt betrayed by our Hindu beliefs, by the double standards. Millions prayed to Kali but no one wanted to *be kali*. Millions of *kali* women were seen as darkness themselves. Their emotions and their being, both deemed insignificant. If Kali and all those women shared the same name and colour, why weren't they given the same respect – or at least a fraction of it?

I had to find the light behind this darkness. There must be some logic to this betrayal because I wasn't satisfied with the answers I had received so far.

20
THE HOLY GRAIL

September 1991, Japan

Mr Hunter, our history teacher, had a look about him. Boring, to put it simply. He had a balding head, wore silver glasses, and walked with a slight hunch. He was barely an inch taller than me. But he surprised me, making our history lessons come alive. He taught passionately, shuffling back and forth from one end of the blackboard to the other. By the end of every class, the blackboard was full of text, diagrams, and timelines. If we had smartphones then, all we would have had to do was click a picture of the board after every lesson. Notes done.

The timing couldn't have been better. We began to learn about Indian history in the new school year, September 1991. And he seemed to know everything. Any time any one of us had questions he rarely referred to the textbook on his desk.

We learned about India being 'the golden bird', one of the richest nations, and how the Aryans, a light-eyed, fair-skinned race invaded India and the local tribes of the Dravidian race, generally dark-skinned, were conquered easily. From the Aryans, the Moguls, the Portuguese, to the British, we learned how India was conquered multiple times, millennia after millennia. We were taught about the caste system and finally, about the British Empire and colonialism.

'Head to the AV room, everyone. We'll be watching the movie *Gandhi* today,' Mr Hunter said just five minutes after he started one lesson. As the rest of the students ambled out of the classroom, half excited, half dreading the long movie, I waited at my desk, watching Mr Hunter wipe the board clean.

I had the urge to ask him about Hindu mythology, but I had learned not to put my foot in my mouth. Mentioning Goddess Kali during lessons would be like scoring an own goal. Things were going well with The Boys. All name-calling had stopped. We ate together, studied in the library together, caught the same train back and forth to school, and even danced together again at parties. What if mentioning Goddess Kali reignited a desire among The Boys to call me names again? What if they didn't let an opportunity like that pass? I didn't fully trust them yet.

'Mr Hunter, when are we going to learn about Hindu mythology?' I asked, seeing him put the duster down. 'Hinduism has so many goddesses I want to learn about and want to understand why and when they came about.'

'Hindu mythology is a minefield,' he replied. 'I'm afraid we won't be covering that.'

'But we covered Greek and Roman mythology briefly when we studied the history of those countries?'

He hesitated for a few moments. 'To be honest, I don't have any knowledge of Hindu mythology. Books in the library would be your best bet,' he said, scratching his bald head.

Books. How I avoided them at all costs, except textbooks. My logic was simple: why did I need to bother with other books if all the learning to be done was in textbooks? I could just ask Mummy and Papa what they knew and avoid books.

After watching *Gandhi*, I understood where elements of white skin privilege and white supremacy came from. But having seen Goddess Kali, I felt that colourism in India seemed somehow much older than colonialism.

That evening at home, I asked both Mummy and Papa about the goddess. Neither knew much more than the priests. Papa could tell I wanted answers, and this was his chance to guide me to his preferred source of knowledge.

'Your school library might have some books on Her?' he said.

'I know what you're trying to do, Papa.'

'Answers to all questions are in books, Shweta.'

'Lord Krishna is *kala* too,' Mummy's voice travelled from the kitchen, along with the aroma of homemade *gulab jamuns*. 'Maybe the *Bhagavad Gita* will have some answers for you.'

'Oh yes! I'm His colour, right?'

'Yes, that's right. Why don't you and I read the *Bhagavad Gita* together?' said Papa. Astounded by the offer, given Papa's atheism, I couldn't possibly reject it. I didn't want to ask for the reason in case he changed his mind. Perhaps he was looking for answers too.

'That's not a bad idea. I need to read a non-fiction book for my English project this year. This could kill two birds with one stone.' *Anything to cut reading time.*

'Dinner is ready. Can we eat quickly? I want to watch the next episode of *Mahabharat*,' said Mummy. The series had been finally released on video. It was an epic based on the greatest battle in India, thousands of years ago, around the time when Lord Krishna had descended to Earth to end evil. The *Bhagavad Gita* was Lord Krishna's spoken words on the battlefield to a great warrior, Arjuna, about duty and the path to salvation.

We nestled into the brown leather sofas as Mummy brought out a plate full of cut fruit, a daily after-dinner spread of apples, oranges, melon and *kaki*.

'Where are the *gulab jamuns*?' I asked, disappointed to see the fruit platter.

'They're not ready yet,' Mummy said, slipping the video cassette into the VCR. Initially, I wasn't interested in the series but if I was going to read the holy scripture, I might as well watch it and learn about Krishna. That way I could skim through the book.

Mummy and Papa had already watched 17 episodes and said that I hadn't missed much. Because I was familiar with this epic tale, it only took a few minutes to work out where we were in the series. Halfway through episode 18, Mummy paused the video and went to the kitchen to fetch a bowl full of *gulab jamuns*. When she returned and played the video again, I reached for a piece straight from the bowl, squeezing the syrup out. On my third piece, I nearly choked at what I saw on the screen. The same scene, a woman bathing under a waterfall. The same woman. The Creepy Man's words - 'Do you bathe like her, Shweta?' - may as well have flashed across the TV screen.

'I have a lot of homework to finish,' I said, coughing my way to my room. Watching sexually arousing scenes together with the family made everyone feel uncomfortable anyway. Mummy and Papa would start chatting about the most random things, like the price of coriander at the local shop, to distract us.

I stopped for a moment. *Shall I tell Mummy? Tell her what The Creepy Man said to me while watching this scene? Maybe then she'll believe me and agree on how inappropriate it was.* But I couldn't bring myself to say it.

Why a religious series would have such a scene baffled me. Perhaps I would learn a little more about life than just the roots of colourism from the *Bhagavad Gita*, I thought.

I finally turned to books, my first read for pleasure being the *Bhagavad Gita As It Is*, a religious scripture. I needed answers and was prepared for anything I could find. And I certainly did learn a lot more than I had expected.

I found a significant part of the scripture shockingly patriarchal, like the fact that women were to be treated like children because they were perceived as less intelligent than men. When I discussed this with Papa, he said that the scripture reflected society thousands of years ago.

The Hindu caste system structured society from the highest to the lowest caste: *Brahmins* (the scholars and priests), *Kshatriyas* (the rulers and warriors), *Vaishyas* (the business class), and the *Sudras* (the manual labourers and servants). This was another social construct I objected to vehemently. More so because it was called the Varna System; the literal meaning of the word *varna* in Sanskrit translates to *colour*. I asked Papa if Hindus were categorised into these castes based on their colour. Papa wasn't sure; again, he put it down to the ways of society then. But I had seen this system, thousands of years old, thriving in Indian society in the twentieth century too. *Brahmins* flashed the white thread around their neck and shoulders, symbolic of their status. *Kshatriyas* boasted about their warrior background and bravery. I discovered that we were *Vaishyas*, not that I cared.

A fifth caste, the *Dalits* (the Untouchables), was added to the system much later. Being treated like an Untouchable for a few days during my monthly cycle infuriated me; I couldn't imagine how the *Dalits* were treated daily. Like Sneha, who cleaned the toilets of the house in Delhi daily. Sneha, only ever dressed in oversized, faded salwar kameez, perhaps donated to her by the families she cleaned for, stood at a distance from the entrance door after ringing the bell. She even used to bring her own broom. Nobody would come near her, let alone touch her. If they did accidentally, they would go straight for a shower.

The principles of *dharma* (your duties according to the caste you're born into) and *karma* (your deeds) were also discussed extensively in the *Bhagavad Gita*. What I found most interesting as a teenager, though, was the preaching of abstinence from any intoxication and sex, which Papa and I never discussed. It turned out that the scene of a woman bathing under a waterfall was a test of a man's desire for his own wife. Even with your own spouse, sex was only to be had for procreation. Other than that, one is meant to continue on their path of *dharma* and control all their desires for salvation.

Screw that! No abstinence for me, thank you.

Watching the *Mahabharat* series, Mummy said that among the 108 names of Krishna, *Shyam*, 'as dark as the night', was one of them; in fact, Krishna's name was derived from the Sanskrit word *Krsna*, meaning 'black'. In photos sold in the shops, Lord Krishna was often depicted as blue-black. Yet in *Mahabharat*, the actor playing Krishna was *gora*. Even in temples, I had only ever seen Krishna's statues made of white marble.

I hadn't found the answers I was looking for. The list of questions, however, was getting longer. One paradox, in particular, bothered me.

'You said Shweta in Sanskrit means *pure, white, fair,* right?' I asked my parents at the dinner table one evening.

'That's right,' they confirmed.

'And Krishna in Sanskrit means black?'

They nodded with mouthfuls of rice and *daal*.

'The verses in the *Bhagavad Gita* are written in Sanskrit. So, if Krishna, black in colour, is described as the Purest Soul, and as the Supreme God, then why is white considered pure? We saw the movie *Gandhi* in school recently. I understand a little about the obsession with fair skin from watching it. But the *Bhagavad Gita* was written thousands of years ago. There was no British rule then.'

Both praised me for the question but neither had any answers.

While I went on to finish the book with Papa, I lost interest in the scripture because instead of answering my questions, it confounded me. Papa, on the other hand, seemed to have found his answers. He had begun to pray regularly.

Encyclopaedias were the next stop. Papa was so thrilled he bought me a brand-new set of the 1991 edition of *Encyclopaedia Britannica*, costing almost as much as a second-hand car! I skimmed through sections of the set, in case I could find answers in them. To my disappointment, in neither the *Bhagavad Gita* nor the encyclopaedias, did I find anything explaining *why* fair skin was considered beautiful.

21

CRASH COURSE

Summer 1993, India

I circled back to where I began – temples. Some knowledgeable priest in some temple should be able to shed light on this darkness, I thought. After all, it was part of their job description: imparting wisdom about God, and in the case of Hinduism, gods and goddesses.

During the summer break of 1993, I tagged along with my aunts or cousins to visit temples, starting with a local temple on the high street in Karol Bagh. As usual, I had my list of questions prepared for the priest. One day, after paying our respects to all the deities, my cousin Mayuri stood ahead of me in the queue to receive the *prasad*. The priest, sitting on a low stool, had a long sandalwood *tilak* on his forehead. It looked fresh, a cool scent lingering near him. He was almost bald but looked after his few remaining strands of hair well, plaiting and resting them on the back of his neck. Recognising my cousin Mayuri, he greeted her with a warm smile.

'Just the holy water, Pundit Ji,' she said, cupping her

hands together after adjusting the veil of her pale blue *salwar kameez*. 'I'm fasting today so I can't have the *prasad*.'

'Fasting? For what?' I asked, queuing up behind her.

'I'm fasting for 16 Mondays. It's for Lord Shiva.'

'What for?'

'For a good husband.'

Before I could process that, a lady behind me commented, 'You're doing the right thing. That fast helped me too. But there's one more thing you need to do.'

The lady, itching to share her wisdom, looked like a newlywed with a mesmerising glow on her face. She wore a deep red sari and heavy gold jewellery. Her red bangles, about two dozen of them on each wrist, clanked as she talked with her hands. I didn't like her intrusion, but this wasn't the first time this had happened in India.

Mayuri was intrigued. She walked towards the lady, signalling for me to move to the side. I followed.

'You look beautiful. Your skin is like a thousand light bulbs turned on at once,' said Mayuri.

'Thank you! I worked hard for this.'

'How? What did you do?'

'I am married to the man of my dreams. We met in college and loved each other. But his mother wasn't happy with my colour. You see, I was *saanvli*, bronze, about a year ago.'

Mayuri and I opened our mouths wide in surprise. This lady could not have been *saanvli*.

'I applied gram flour and yoghurt body packs for more than three months, daily. I also stopped going out in the sun.

You'll achieve fair skin in no time, given you're *ghehuan,* wheatish.'

'What? Mayuri, I think you are *gori,'* I corrected the lady.

'I wish I was. I still need to improve my colour. It's not as *saaf,* clean, as this beautiful lady.'

'What do you mean by *saaf?* Darker skin tone is seen as dirty?'

Mayuri ignored me, determined to learn as many tips as possible from this lady.

'What's my colour then, according to you both?'

Mayuri said *kali* and the stranger said *saanvli* at the same time.

'Wow, I didn't think there was any confusion about my colour until now.'

'You're not that dark. But because your parents are very fair, the colour contrast to others makes you appear *kali,*' Mayuri replied, justifying her answer.

Partaking in the surreal conversation that day, I learned that every Indian had a PhD in Fairology. But the four major readings on the Fairometer were open to interpretation. A *gori* to someone could be a *ghehuan* to another. I was *kali* to one but *saanvli* to another. It was all relative. A farcical, man-made concept.

The two of them continued to talk about colour and remedies to achieve a lighter skin tone. And with such ease, as though they were discussing wall paint.

'The most effective remedy of all is. . .'

'The cream,' Mayuri and the lady said in unison.

'Yes! It really works. A year later, I am now married to my lover and couldn't be happier.'

I had tried using the fairness cream myself in a desperate attempt to climb up the Fairometer, but that didn't stop me from lecturing the lady – because she was a stranger.

'Don't you worry that if your mother-in-law rejected you for your colour, she may have other demands? You really want to spend your life with a family who places this much importance on your complexion?'

'Shweta!' said Mayuri, gawking at me in anger. She stepped forward to cover me.

'It's OK. I'm not offended,' the lady said, looking me in the eye. 'There is no escape from colour so there's no point in making a big deal of it either. My parents and I, reluctantly, met several suitors after the mother-in-law-to-be had rejected me. You know what happened? Most other suitors did too. And I wasn't keen on those who liked me. If 'improving' my colour is the only thing I must do to marry the man of my dreams, I don't think there's anything wrong with that.'

As Mayuri and this lady continued exchanging tips, a slim, tall man approached them. Wrapping his arms around the lady, he said, 'Shall we go now?' His warm smile lit up both faces. A couple madly in love.

'Wait a minute. . .'

Mayuri pinched me before I could utter a word. She had read my mind. This man's skin tone was the same as mine. Why did men pass unscathed by colourism while women were expected to meet certain colour standards?

Before leaving, the lady imparted one last word of wisdom, whispering in Mayuri's ear.

'What did she say to you?'

'You're too young to know.'

'Oh please, I know everything, OK?'

'She's pregnant. And she gave me some tips on the kind of foods to have and to avoid when I expect a baby. Foods that will help me have a fair baby.'

'Please stop! Enough of this obsession! It's your qualities and personality that should matter. When will this ever stop if we worry about the colour of an unborn child?'

'Of course, it is wrong. But this is how life is here in India, in the real world. Come out of your Bollywood dream world in which falling in love is normal. Most of us have arranged marriages. So, we might as well have the best shot at being attractive, hence having more of a choice in picking *our* life partner,' said Mayuri. She charged out of the temple hastily while I tried to keep up with her pace and her responses.

She stopped and turned. 'And I suggest you start with the remedies, given your colour. You're pretty for a dark girl. Imagine how much prettier you could be, fairer. I'll be married soon and off to a new life. I'm saying this as your cousin who cares for you.'

Her words stung. Mayuri was nineteen and her parents were actively looking for a suitor to get her married. In fact, most of my cousins were mentally preparing themselves from the age of sixteen for matrimony, acquiescing to introductions by their families. Amma, my paternal grandmother, had mentioned in passing to my parents that I didn't need a university education. She often suggested they should start considering proposals for me. I was fifteen then. Papa and Mummy had no such plans. A university degree was the least they wanted for me. But that's not to say that minds could not be changed. That was my worry, anyway.

I was pulled back down to reality. Trying to fight colourism in India was like trying to swim out of a whirlpool: impossible, barring a miraculous force propelling you out, i.e., a mass revolution. Having understood their plight, I felt guilty for judging my cousins. I was confused myself, still teetering on that seesaw. Now, more than confused, I was genuinely concerned about what my biodata would say about my colour. What kind of an ordeal my parents would have to go through to get me married to a suitable boy of *my* choice? The way I was starting to see things, if you were dark and hoping for a marriage proposal then 'beggars can't be choosers.'

I ran through an entire 'first meeting' scene in my head. I had seen plenty of those in the movies. Prospective families would come over for tea with their sought-after bachelor son. They would have already seen my airbrushed photo in the biodata, lightened with make-up and blinding white studio lights. They would be impressed by my parents and their colour. Then I would enter the room, draped in a sari, shuffling slowly with a tray in my hands, hot masala chai and samosas capturing their attention first. Of course, I wouldn't drink chai. Maya Mami had once said, 'You shouldn't drink tea if you're already dark. It will make you darker.' I'd only serve it to the others. When they would shift their attention to me, they wouldn't be able to hide their disappointment, especially having seen my parents. And they would leave. No questions necessary – the swift departure would say it all.

If there was any contact by the suitor's family again, it would be a conditional offer. Asking for a dowry was unfashionable but expecting lavish gifts wasn't. A new luxury car, an opulent wedding in a five-star hotel, a down payment for a new apartment, gold or diamond gifts for all the relatives of the groom – these were some popular choices for gifts in exchange for taking your daughter. And if the daughter was dark, the list of gifts lengthened right in front of your eyes.

I couldn't put my parents through that. It was time to give that fairness cream another shot. Either that or I needed to start with the Sixteen-Mondays fast myself.

I had forgotten about asking the priest why Goddess Kali is *kali*. I didn't care anymore about the roots of colourism. What bothered me was how sexism manifested itself in that belief system. Although Krishna is supposed to be *kala* as per all the religious scripts, somewhere along the way, He began to be depicted as fair-skinned. But Kali was always *kali*. Although this dichotomy vexed me, I started to feel that being Blackie, as a female, *was* a big deal. My future depended on it. And apparently, so did the future of my unborn child.

The Fairometer crash course eight years earlier had me questioning my career aspirations, shattering my dreams of becoming a Bollywood actress. The discussion today made me anxious about my future choices of a partner.

22

SIXTEEN MONDAYS

September 1993, Japan

Fasting for sixteen Mondays worked. Not for a husband. I made a boyfriend, sort of.

Between the two options of using fairness creams or fasting, fasting was much easier. How much fairer could I get from the cream anyway? Besides, the effect of the cream would be temporary, whereas the effect of fasting to appease the Almighty surely would be permanent.

Although I didn't believe in fasting, wanting a life partner of my choice was a fundamental desire. The way my cousins were getting married off, my time wasn't far away. After reading the *Bhagavad Gita As It Is,* I started to become uncomfortable with many elements of the Hindu religion and the patriarchy deeply embedded in several teachings. Like the fact that there were countless female goddesses in the religion, yet I only ever saw male priests in temples. I was told female priests were considered 'impure' because of their monthly menstrual cycle.

The more I had been investigating, the more I disapproved of the loopholes in the customs in the name of religion.

But, for selfish reasons, pleasing the Gods to secure a good husband seemed like a wise choice. The fast was meant to be in honour of Lord Shiva, but I prayed with Goddess Kali in mind, holding Her responsible for my happiness. Of all the thousands of Hindu gods and goddesses, She ought to empathise with me. Not just empathise – She represented all the dark-skinned girls. *She* was our ambassador.

Before I embarked on this fasting journey, I wanted to make sure I could cope. I still had a big appetite, and with teenage hormones raging through my body, I was ravenous by 11 a.m. most days when lunch wasn't served until 1 p.m. at school.

Thanks to all the baking I was doing, a new hobby, I was starting to grow horizontally too. I used diet control as an excuse when Mummy asked me why I wanted to fast. Who was I fooling? She knew of the Sixteen-Mondays fast. Besides, I didn't want to be dark *and* overweight. I was already conspicuous for my colour; the last thing I wanted was to also be 'the plump one' amongst slender Japanese teenagers.

In September 1993, aged sixteen, I tightened my school skirt every Monday, clicking the clasp on the tightest setting. Fasting was on. I was allowed to have milk, fruits, and nuts all day if I wanted, but I could eat a substantial meal of grains and pulses only once a day – a piece of cake. However, even after grazing on nuts and fruits all day, I used to return home famished. I would eat twice the amount I normally ate for dinner, leaving my plate sparkling clean. The diet element of fasting didn't work. But I stuck with it and did not cheat. Not even once.

With fasting on Mondays becoming a background routine, I focused on excelling at schoolwork and my grades.

An impressive GPA meant a better chance of admission to a university in the US. It would be quite a stretch for the family, financially. But, if I did well, perhaps I could change their mind to my benefit.

Maths and science teachers encouraged me to take Advancement Placement Math and Biology. I was brilliant at them. I also found computer programming a breeze, and I was passionate about International Relations. I joined the school debating team and became a class rep for The Student Council. One of my favourite parts about being a class rep was reading all announcements for a week on the school PA.

My proudest moment of all came when my school hosted the Model United Nations. Preparing for an entire year to represent a country and debate resolutions in the United Nations setting was not only intellectually stimulating but thrilling too. Thrilling because a few other schools participated; pupils unaware of my backstory only saw me as a confident and ambitious chatterbox.

My grades reflected my hard work as I surpassed the 4.0 GPA mark for the first time. My body, undergoing hormonal changes, gave me a fuller figure, and finally, I made it into the A team in the girls' soccer club! I made a mean defender. Perhaps this was all part of Goddess Kali's plan – to help me if I helped myself.

None of this beat getting some attention from boys, the teenage barometer for one's attractiveness. One afternoon, in the school library (yes, I was now visiting the library and actually reading), Yoshi, a popular Japanese boy from my class, pulled my bra strap from behind. Intelligent, sporty and ever so charming, he was every girl's crush. I didn't rebuke him. I should have flinched. Instead, my cheeks began radiating heat and the hair on the back of my neck stood erect. Although I did turn around to give him a disapproving look, my heart was racing. The words 'How dare you?!' never came out.

Whatever came over him, I savoured that moment. I felt attractive because he didn't have The Creepy Man's lustful gaze. Taking my speechlessness as approval, he asked, 'Hey Shwetz, what's your bra size?'

'Yoshi!'

'All right, just tell me your cup size?'

'Stop it! Is this one of your stupid dares?'

Asking girls in the class for their bra size had become a popular dare in class. Sometimes, they brazenly guessed sizes out loud as girls walked into the classroom. I had never imagined I would be one of those girls. The girls didn't pay too much attention to the boys' comments. We blamed their hormones and the sexual influences surrounding us. Magazines full of topless women were accessible in every Lawson convenience store. After school, boys from our class regularly loitered in the magazine aisle of a Lawson near Suma station; Love Hotels, where rooms were rented by the hour, were dotted around the city; the scripts of primetime TV programmes were filled with sexual innuendo – minus the innuendo. Even a child could work out the double meaning behind all the dialogue.

The sixteen Mondays of fasting ended in January of the following year. In March, the family visited Singapore for Chaya's wedding. Chaya was Papa's elder brother's daughter. Bade Papa looked exactly like Papa, a slimmer version without a double chin. Even their voices were often mistaken for each other's. Chaya, twenty-years-old, was about to tie the knot. As happy as I was for her, I didn't want that for myself. My prayers to Goddess Kali always started with, 'I trust that you will give me a good husband. Only when I'm ready.'

She gave me the next best thing in the interim. One of the wedding events was a mid-afternoon civilised bachelorette party. It included the family's older ladies, and no alcohol was served. I happened to be performing to a song – which, ironically, contained the word *goria* – when Chaya's brother Sohan and his friend took a sneak peek. Flustered, my heart skipped a beat, as Sohan's friend – a slim, handsome boy with sexy sideburns – watched me intently. As soon as I finished, Sohan ambled into the room as a messenger.

'My friend Vipin wants to talk to you,' he said, eyes pinned to the floor, reluctant and uncomfortable. Ever since the juice bar incident in Delhi the previous summer, things had become a little awkward between us. That summer, Sohan and I would jaunt up and down the local high street every day. We used to make each other laugh with our similar sense of humour. We were of a similar age too, only five months apart. Those two were the only similarities. By 6 p.m., as the temperature dropped from 45 degrees to 35 degrees, we would head to a juice bar at the end of the high street. One day, we were more than halfway down the road when I paused upon hearing a loud whistle.

I always reacted to catcalling, wanting to catch a glance at the boy(s). I looked up to see two raucous teenagers, in garish half-sleeved shirts, leaning against a dilapidated scooter. 'You think we're interested in you? Wishful thinking. Not you, him,' they scoffed.

Sohan didn't stop. 'Come on, Shweta, keep walking.'

'Oi, *firang*, foreigner,' said the teenagers. 'Your standard has dropped, don't you think? Why are you with her?'

Sohan ignored them. His grey-green eyes stared straight ahead at nothing. He grabbed my arm, his pale, fair hand with golden hairs against my brown arm, urging me to walk faster. Sohan was often mistaken for a *firang* and given preferential treatment in shops and restaurants. 'We can give you a special table here,' restaurant managers would tell him. 'How will you pay, sir? In *Umrican* dollars?' Even as a fifteen-year-old, he was often addressed as 'sir'. It was amusing how they presumed he was American. Even more amusing was the reaction when people discovered he was Indian and spoke fluent Hindi.

The boys sat on the scooter, riding at a slow pace alongside us.

'What's the matter, *firang*? Didn't find anyone else to be with?'

'Shut up! She's my cousin,' said Sohan.

'We all say, that don't we? Brother by day, lover by night,' they said scornfully.

'How dare you?!' Sohan let go of my hand immediately, his eyes turning from grey-green to steel-grey with anger. I pulled his arm and pleaded with him to ignore the boys. We continued walking to the juice bar. The boys smirked, knowing that their provocation had worked. I don't remember anything else they said. It couldn't have been worse than what had already been said. Eventually, they turned around, afraid we might ask for help.

At the juice bar, the owner started preparing our favourite juice – a mix of grapefruits, oranges, and carrots with a pinch of Himalayan salt. He stole glances at us, curiously observing the silence between Sohan and me. Dead-still, hot air, drowned the honks of vehicles, cows mooing, stray dogs barking, and the shoppers bargaining with shopkeepers. Although the juice was prepared just the way we liked it, I felt nauseous with the first sip, disgusted by the incident. Sohan, antsy, sipped half-heartedly.

'Let's go home,' he said. We paid for our unfinished drinks and left the juice bar, Sohan walking ahead, me a few steps behind, processing.

Papa's entire family is fair. His parents, four siblings, and their children. All of them. One walking ahead of me - an Indian who looks Caucasian - is blessed with 'Umrican' genes. Why was I picked to be cursed with dark skin? And why the only one? An anomaly.

The juice bar visits stopped. This incident introduced a slight awkwardness in our relationship, the kind that lingers when two people choose not to discuss an issue, a mutual, unspoken agreement.

That day at the bachelorette party, Sohan delivered the news about Vipin's interest and scampered out on the last word. Vipin and I chatted all night through many of the wedding events, exchanging flirtatious glances and smiles. He told me I danced well and that he liked my smile. A month after I returned to Kobe, I found a thick, white envelope in our letterbox addressed to me. I rushed up to our apartment on the sixth floor and darted straight to my room.

'*Gulab jamuns*, Shweta?' Mummy asked from the kitchen.

'In a bit,' I said, ripping open the envelope. A four-page, handwritten letter on lined paper.

'It's the first time the aroma of *gulab jamuns* hasn't tempted you. You normally eat five or six straight out of the saucepan,' Mummy said, entering my room abruptly with two *gulab jamuns* in a bowl. I quickly sat on the letter. She placed the bowl on my desk and left.

When I started reading the letter, Vipin's blue-inked words – dipped in romance and sweeter than the syrup of *gulab jamuns* – floated in my diminutive room. He said all he had done was think about me since the wedding. I must have read the letter a few hundred times. Out of all the gorgeous teenagers at the wedding, he fancied me. Standing in front of my dressing table mirror, I wondered what he saw in me. How could I have drawn someone towards me to that extent? We connected, *and* he had been missing me for a whole month. What did he see?

I wanted so badly to ask him that. Sitting at my mahogany desk, I pulled out a notepad and started writing, 'Dearest Vipin'. I traced over the two words again. I stopped. I couldn't find the words to articulate myself. Unlike him, I didn't have a way with words. Unimpressed by my response to his amorous letter, I didn't want him to break it off. I stuck the letter within my biology textbook and took it to school, hoping to get some tips from Sarina.

'Wow, Shwetz! He's totally into you,' Sarina said, scanning the letter in the school toilet while several girls were busy preening themselves, rolling their skirts up, redoing their high ponytails, smearing more lip gloss.

'What does he look like? How old is he?'

'Fifteen.'

'He's romantic, all right.'

'How are you going to reply?'

'Can you help me write it?'

'Ha, you want *me* to help you write a love letter to express *your* feelings? You're on your own for this one. It's not a book review.' In previous years, I had often coaxed Sarina into sharing her summer reading book reviews with me. *Around the World in 80 Days*, *The Hobbit,* and *Anne Frank's Diary* are just a few books that come to mind.

It took me more than a week to write two pages. I don't remember what I wrote but I do remember asking for a photo. He sent me one, looking delicious, and asked for mine. I didn't want to send any. What if he changed his mind after seeing a photo? I would rather he remembered me the way he saw me at the wedding. I reluctantly sent one. Then began the waiting game. We would exchange letters and save our pocket money to buy a phone card just to speak to each other for a total of five minutes. I was enamoured by his charm. I had a pen-pal boyfriend, and I wanted to announce it to my school during the daily announcements on the PA.

Good Morning,

It is Monday 30th May 1994. This is Shweta Khandelwal from 11th-grade. Can I have your attention for the following important announcements today?

– Unfortunately, the after-school music club today has been cancelled.

– The Girls' Soccer team played The Canadian Academy over the weekend and made us proud by winning 4–2.

– Shweta Khandelwal, that's right, the Blackie, has a dashing, tall, and very romantic boyfriend, with sexy sideburns, in Singapore.

Have a great day!

Aside from my close friends, I didn't share my relationship status with anyone. If The Boys found out, they could accuse me of inventing a make-believe boyfriend for attention. They could claim I wrote the letters myself and that the boy in the photo was probably one of my cousins. I still didn't trust them entirely. Just as well that I didn't because come June, after somehow convincing my parents that I should go to Singapore and not India for the summer holidays, Vipin and I broke up. He declared that it wouldn't work, given the distance. We hadn't even held hands or kissed. Does a romantic pen-pal count as a boyfriend?

The most obscure of romantic relationships came and went in a flash. It hurt when it ended but it left behind the most coveted memento – self-confidence. Nothing could go wrong now. If only I had known, it wasn't just my self-confidence, my whole world was about to be shaken.

23

5.46 A.M.

January 1995, Japan

Kobe was a sleepy city – living and breathing, but sleepy. It made its presence felt every now and then with occasional, gentle sways of the ground beneath us. Failing to acknowledge the sways as a harbinger of a greater catastrophe, we continued to call Kobe sleepy.

At 5:46 a.m. on 17 January 1995, the city reacted violently to that description. It roared and performed an angry dance. The first half of the performance felt like a terrible nightmare, with the entire city fast asleep during the early hours of the morning. As the ground continued to shake, almost a metre left and right, I reached for my bunk bed bars on both sides.

'Please don't fall on Neeraj below me,' I chanted in my head.

I screamed for my brother, but the deafening roar stifled my voice. He probably screamed too, in vain. Entire buildings were swaying, some collapsing, some set on fire instantly. Every utensil in the kitchen was clanking, glassware shattering. Enormous tidal waves crashed against Kobe's port. Parked vehicles were engulfed by roads that had been ripped open. Delivery trucks collided with other vehicles on the move. Trains derailed. Mountains split. All at the same time, it sounded as if it was raining bombs. Except that it wasn't an enemy attacking us. It was our very own city.

We had practised earthquake drills in school several times, but a drill never comes close to preparing you for reality. Not at 5:46 a.m., caught completely off guard. I knew exactly what we were experiencing and prayed that Mummy and Papa in their bedroom weren't injured, or worse . . . dead.

Twenty seconds of the most devastating earthquake Kobe has ever witnessed, recorded at 7.3 on the Richter scale. Twenty seconds. It only takes a second to die in a natural disaster. Surviving twenty seconds was nothing short of a miracle.

The tremor stopped just as abruptly as it had started. I waited for my adrenaline to take charge, but instead of jumping off the bunk bed in search of Mummy and Papa, I lay stupefied. Fear held me back, a fear of seeing something terrible.

'Didi?' said Neeraj, his voice quivering.

'Neeraj! Are you OK?' I was relieved that my bed hadn't fallen on him.

'Didi, I want to go to Mummy and Papa.'

'No! Don't move from the bed. We don't know what state the apartment is in outside this room,' I said. 'Stay right there. I'll come down to your bed.'

I said that without any intention of climbing down, petrified myself. We were safe. For the time being. And that was all that mattered at that moment. One moment at a time. For all I knew, there could be nothing outside our bedroom door. Our very own building could be split in half.

Then our door rattled. Papa barged in, then Mummy.

'Neeraj? Shweta? Are you both OK?' Papa peered through the bunk bed bars in the dark. OK? Imagine someone putting you on the most dangerous rollercoaster ride while you are fast asleep. Imagine how you would feel by the end of that ride. I was aware of every cell in my body, aware of the blood and adrenaline running through my veins, aware that this was far worse than a rollercoaster because there was no safety belt and no guarantee that I would be alive at the end of the ride.

Papa helped me down, Mummy grabbed Neeraj. A pile of clothes had been thrown out of the mahogany wardrobe, books flung from the desk shelf, wardrobe doors and desk drawers open, as though the room had been ransacked.

Wide-eyed, we held hands and moved in single file. Every step closer to the apartment door was a gamble. Each step could be our last, the building crumbling into rubble. The kitchen on the left, the open-plan living room to our right, nothing seemed damaged. Not that we took time to examine anything. The shoe cabinet by the door had toppled, blocking our exit route. Papa held the cabinet up while we passed through, and Mummy grabbed the keys.

We shouldn't have taken the elevator down to the ground floor, but that didn't occur to us then. We exited the building and fled barefoot to the private car park 25 metres away. We were safe but cold. At -3 degrees centigrade, it was a frigid morning. We huddled in the car park in nothing but our pyjamas.

'The car! The car will keep us warm,' Papa said.

It hadn't even been a minute when the ground shook again, jolting the car.

'Out of the car now!' Papa hollered, worried about the car engine malfunctioning with such a jolt, or the doors getting jammed.

'We're going to freeze to death in the cold. We must go back to get our jackets and shoes,' Mummy insisted.

'I'll go. You all stay here,' Papa said.

'Anywhere we go, we go together,' Mummy replied.

This time we took the wrought-iron, spiral staircase to the sixth floor. Mummy and Papa went inside the apartment, instructing Neeraj and me to stay outside. Papa grabbed his wallet by his bedside table, Mummy rummaged through the shoe cabinet and jackets hanging on the pegs above it.

Second time lucky, we made it back to the car park. An open space was the safest place, yet nothing felt safe anymore. Our only solace was that we were all together, still alive. Other families trickled out of their homes, everyone looking startled. Strangely, things around us seemed intact, making us doubt our own assumptions about the experience. No broken buildings, no ripped roads, no flipped cars.

'That was a big earthquake, right?' Everyone asked each other the same question. Papa suggested joining friends down the road to check they were safe. But how could we move even an inch when the ground beneath us couldn't be trusted? A ground still grumbling, still angry. Maybe it was all in our heads that the ground was still shaking. Maybe it really did tremble countless times. Reluctantly, we followed Papa's lead.

As we descended downhill, the level of destruction increased. Lawson looked like it had been turned upside down. There was a tear in the road, three metres long, half a metre wide and at least a metre deep. More and more people came out of their apartments, panicked and stone-cold. Tilted electricity poles looked ready to fall in the gentlest breeze; buildings looked perfect at first sight but on closer inspection appeared to be leaning. At any sight of a person, Japanese or Indian, Papa greeted them with a nod, asking if they were OK instead of the usual, '*Ohaiyo gozai masu*, good morning.' There was nothing good about the morning. But still, the wreckage didn't look *so* bad. Not yet.

We found our family friends huddled together in the car park closest to them, all numb. The ladies hugged each other and shed tears of joy on seeing one another. The men shook hands, greeting each other with just one question, 'All OK with the apartment?' A futile question, given that the fate of every structure depended on the frequency and intensity of more tremors.

Another aftershock struck, and we all screamed in unison. At least there were more of us now. We felt safer.

A lot of *surviving* happened between 6 a.m. and 6 p.m. The order of events is a little jumbled up in my mind: how we survived every aftershock, hundreds of them; how we kept ourselves warm; how and what we ate, if at all, and where we were going to stay.

One by one, car parks started to fill up with people, desperate and aghast, wrapped up in all sorts of bedding. No one knew what to do, how long to stay out, or what their future held in store for them. All we could do was wait for dawn to provide some warmth and expose the real damage. And wait for Prime Minister Tomiichi Murayama to guide us. Where were the basic necessities – food, water, and shelter – going to come from? The earthquake left a bountiful city destitute.

A little later that morning the government spurred into action. Police patrols kept us all informed, their faces telling the stories of countless homeless souls, their shoulders carrying the weight of sorrow of every family in their jurisdiction.

'Do not enter your buildings, your homes, no matter how safe they may appear,' said one patrolman.

The government officials started handing out *onigiris* (Japanese rice and dried seaweed parcels), water, and biscuits at multiple crossroads. When the head of Lawson Supermarkets announced that all earthquake victims could help themselves to anything in any Lawson in Kobe, people queued with commendable poise. No one swept the shelves clean. In fact, most even left some money on the cashier counters. The Yakuzas, the Japanese mafia, also came to the rescue, serving people water and milk for children. I believe opening school halls was one of the government's instructions. The Japanese started to congregate in these halls, hundreds of them, while many Indians huddled in The India Club.

Papa called his elder brother, Bade Papa, in Singapore from a green public telephone booth, which was thankfully still working. A surreal conversation took place between them. It seemed that the rest of the world had come to know about the severity of the disaster before us. Kobe made it onto the international news after all. Bade Papa had already seen it on the morning news and had been eagerly waiting for our call.

'There are blazing fires in a large area,' he said. 'Something like Shin-Nagata?'

Marist, my school, was a couple of train stops past Shin-Nagata. I was reminded of my school, my teachers, and my classmates. I hadn't seen any of my friends either. When Sarina ambled past our car park, I ran to hug her.

'How are the rest? Sunaina, Meena, Ambika, Faiza? And The Boys?' I asked, my teeth chattering in the cold.

'Everyone's fine. Nikhil's building is on fire. I am going to see him.'

I looked at Mummy for permission. Hesitant at first, she nodded. 'Don't hang around or go anywhere else,' she warned.

Nikhil stood on the main road, a blanket wrapped around him, grey clouds of smoke enveloping his building. The despair in his eyes was as painful to endure as the fright from another tremor. His building was only a block further down the hill from ours, the destruction now too close to home. We asked him how he was – a silly question that deserved nothing more than a nod. We felt as helpless as he did as we stood by his side, silently conveying solidarity. I studied his eyes, wondering which possessions in his apartment he would save, given a chance. Perhaps his gaming station and his books. I wondered what I would save if it were my building. Nothing came to mind other than Vipin's letters.

'Have you heard from the school?' I asked Sarina on our way back to the car park.

'Nothing yet. I hope all the teachers in Port Island are safe,' Sarina replied. Port Island, a man-made island off mainland Kobe, was bound to have faced the wrath of the earthquake ten-fold. Add to that a couple of tsunamis and the destruction on the island could be catastrophic.

Our next update came from the Jatias, one of the family friends in our group. They were in India at the time, leaving their large two-storey house in Rokko, higher up in the mountains, vacant. They always left behind a set of keys with Mr Sharma, a distant relative of theirs, and our family friend.

'A kilometre of the Hanshin Express Highway has toppled over. A bus is hanging off the broken highway,' Mr Jatia informed Mr Sharma during another conversation at a public phone booth.

Up until now, we hadn't been able to build a picture of the destruction due to the paucity of information. Now, the impact of the catastrophe had started to sink in, and it terrified us. Even then, the men from the group meandered through the streets of Kobe, in a southward direction, to assess the wreckage. The further south they went, the ghastlier the scene. More and more people roamed the streets, like tourists on a Hollywood movie set. Some even took photos, which surprised me. There was nothing I wanted to remember about the day.

'It's bad, really bad,' the men said upon their return. 'We are lucky to be alive.'

Indeed, our group was fortunate. Mr Tiwari, the size of a sumo wrestler, owned an Indian provision store in the building opposite the car park. The men went in and returned with a portable gas canister, a saucepan, and paper cups. Never mind food – how could Indians survive a day without *chai*?! Some tea and biscuits were all we had all day. Whenever sleep and hunger threatened to visit, another aftershock shooed them away.

'Shouldn't we join the others in The India Club? There is a bigger gathering of the Gujaratis there,' suggested Mrs Sharma.

I asked Papa if he had heard anything about Kanika's family. He said they were safe and taking shelter in the Indian Social Society Club. This club was run mostly by the Sindhis; Kanika belonged to this ethnic group.

'As long as these aftershocks continue, open space is the safest place to be. The police patrols said there will be many more until the plates settle,' said Mr Sharma.

As though right on cue, another aftershock struck. It was these dreaded aftershocks that caused most of the damage. We eventually lost count of how many we experienced. Weakened structures met with a final blow. The appearance of dusk called for a plan other than spending the night in a car park because the temperature had started to plummet.

None of us could return to our apartments; the Jatias offered their house for all of us to take shelter. Once again, everyone went back to their apartments to pack their bags. With every visit, we felt braver yet still fearful, an effect that comes with risk-taking. A handful of clothes and toiletries were enough. No one planned for anything beyond a couple of days. Having said that, passports were packed too. Mr Tiwari packed lots of processed food, lentils, and rice. By 6 p.m. we all gathered in the Jatias' residence, our cars crammed in their basement car park. Surprisingly, the electricity supply hadn't been cut off there. While the ladies turned on the heating, the men turned on the television to the

NHK news channel. As if the updates during the day weren't enough. They had read the book and now wanted to watch the movie.

Sixteen of us gathered around the TV, watching in anguish as our beloved city burned and turned to rubble. It wasn't a scene from a Hollywood movie, it was far worse; it was real. Real people were dead, thousands of them. Real people were made homeless instantaneously. Despite not having had a decent meal in twelve hours, witnessing the devastation extinguished our hunger. But we ate half-heartedly.

That night, all sixteen of us slept crammed in the living room, the rest of the four bedrooms empty. The tremors were relentless. Uncountable. The news on TV had confirmed hundreds of them and warned there would be more to come. We abided by an unspoken promise in the group: we live together, we die together.

Two days later, it became clear that we needed to escape Japan.

'Shweta's passport is missing,' said Papa, holding three in his hands. 'We'll have to go back to the apartment.'

'Why do we need passports? Where are we going?' I asked.

'Singapore.'

My heart sank. Six months ago, I had cunningly managed a visit to Singapore to see Vipin. We weren't together anymore, but he was still Sohan's best friend.

'Why can't we go to India?'

'I'll explain later. Do you know where your passport is?'

'It's with the school, remember? Our school trip to Guam was planned for the end of January.' How I was looking forward to that trip. Nine whole days. The class of 1995 was the first one to have been given permission for the longest trip away. Our class had never been more unified. All name-calling and teasing had ceased. The boys and the girls were inseparable now. We went to Harbour Land together. Sauntered aimlessly through Sannomiya together. Squeezed into karaoke booths together. Got competitive in bowling alleys together. Visited Ikuta Shrine on New Year's Eve together. Ate under Sakura trees during the festival of Hanami together. The trip to Guam would have been nothing but fun and frolics. Now it would undoubtedly be cancelled.

'We'll just have to apply for a new passport in Osaka then,' said Papa.

The next morning, on the 20th, the entire group left for Osaka, in convoy, with just one suitcase for each family of four. The Hanshin Express Highway was closed entirely. We drove on a city road beneath the highway. A journey that used to take one hour took ten.

'Why can't we go to India, Papa?' I raised the question again in the car, gazing out the window, studying the section of the highway that had toppled.

'It'll be a lot easier for me to manage my business from Singapore. Mummy and I will be coming back to Kobe in a week. We'll get you kids back here when school starts.'

I didn't ask again, careful not to plant the seed of suspicion in my parents' minds. Neither knew about my romantic pen pal relationship with Vipin and my heartbreak.

When we arrived at a weekly rental apartment in Osaka,

we called shotgun for the shower. In Kobe, water had been fetched from the mountains in Rokko, which we used sparingly for drinking, cooking, and washing over three days.

We spent a week in Osaka, waiting for the Indian High Commission to issue me a new passport. While the three of them counted down to Singapore, I kept wishing for Papa to change his mind.

You should be grateful to be escaping to a warm country, to the luxury of a four-bedroom apartment and a beautiful pool, a haven in one of the poshest areas in Singapore. All those homeless Japanese people, all those who have lost loved ones, have nowhere to escape.

I'd faced death and survived; facing an ex-boyfriend became the least of my concerns – until I reached Singapore. The first time I met Vipin's new girlfriend, the agony was unbearable. Carrying a broken heart at seventeen hurt more than carrying the memories of a broken city. His girlfriend was strikingly beautiful, the kind of person you would stop to take a second glance at. Her complexion was a creamy latte: warm, flawless, and far lighter than mine. I wished Vipin had never written to me. It felt worse to be stripped of self-confidence after having tasted it than never having it in the first place. But I swallowed my sorrow. Every time Sohan went out with his friends, how could I not go? If I didn't, I would appear vulnerable. When I did, every second spent watching Vipin being intimate with his girlfriend fuelled my complex. Just when I thought I had extinguished it forever, it came back, stronger than ever, like the flame on a magic candle that re-ignites no matter how many times you blow to put it out. I was beginning to run out of air.

'You're alive!' The entire class, seventeen of us, leapt up to give Ryo a group hug.

School resumed a whole month after the earthquake; the building was split in half down the middle of the semi-hexagon. Our apartment building was labelled green – green, orange, red, and black were the colours used to signify the safety level of every building in Kobe. Marist was labelled black. Within a month, prefabricated structures were put up in the playground.

Gaps in Kobe's landscape reminded us of the catastrophe. There were now car parks where buildings once stood. The daily train ride past Sannomiya station to Suma sent chills down our spines. Kobe City station to Shin-Nagata had suffered the most destruction. The Japanese government had done a phenomenal job of clearing up after the earthquake. There were no traumatic sights, but seeing an entire region laid waste was somehow worse, a reminder of the hundreds of lives that had been lost in an instant. Close to 6,000 people died in the earthquake, which had more than 600 recorded aftershocks.[4]

Ryo still hadn't attended school a month after we started. Because there was no news from his family, we feared the worst. When he made his late entrance, Ryo had everyone's undivided attention for the first and probably the only time in the six years at Marist. He was a petite, timid boy who kept to himself and a couple of friends. He rarely answered questions in class, steered clear of any arguments or taking sides, and rarely had a story to tell on Monday mornings when the class exchanged notes about the weekend. He always wore the sweetest smile, though. Now, he had a story like none other. The class circled him, as little children do during story time, and listened intently.

'My house was destroyed. We lived in Kobe City, Nada ward. The ground floor, where we ran our family restaurant, collapsed. We lived on the first floor. My Dad was going to take a shower on the ground floor and got stuck there,' he said.

'How did he manage to get out?' asked a classmate while the rest gasped.

'His friend helped us. He sawed through a wall with a little saw. It took him eight hours.'

'Didn't any firemen come to help?'

'Firemen couldn't keep up with thousands of other emergencies in our area,' Ryo said, pausing to catch his breath.

'After that, we moved around a lot. At first, I stayed at my cousin's house for a few days. Then we moved to my grandma's house in Osaka. Then to another cousin's house in Mie. Then to a friend's house for a few days. And finally, to another grandmother's house, which was also half destroyed. It was next to my house.'

'All these relocations sound exhausting,' said Nikhil. 'Makes sense why you didn't come to school all this time.' He quickly slipped in his story about his move to Osaka. Because repair work was in full swing in his building after the fire, he commuted from Osaka to Suma for two hours each way, to attend school.

'No, it wasn't because of that,' continued Ryo. 'Seeing the destruction in our area, we didn't think school was on. A friend happened to be in my area when I was too. And that's how I found out about school.'

He finished his story, but we still stood circling him,

199

taking it all in. The hardships he had endured, his nomadic life for a couple of months. Such is the wrath of a natural disaster: its effect lingers for months and the memory of the experience, forever.

For the remaining few months before graduation, we all soldiered through, working the hardest we ever had to catch up with the curriculum. We played hard too. Never mind the cancelled trip to Guam. There was a lot of laughter in our class, frequent Saturday night socialising, abundant hugs, lots of tears at the graduation, and heart-warming messages in yearbooks.

There is nothing like a good earthquake to inspire you. Such life-changing incidents come with epiphanies, encouraging you to readjust your core values. Cast, creed, or colour shouldn't matter anymore. Shouldn't.

24
DÉJÀ VU
August 1995, India

Alas, my colour complex was deep-rooted by then. The Wicked Man was silenced by Papa. Forcing Angad to look at his reflection provided some respite. Readjusting core values after a near-death experience should have erased my skin-tone complex. But it was a little too late. Colourism had gotten under my skin. I survived boarding school, a child's worst nightmare at the age of six, and I survived a natural disaster, yet it was my colour complex that broke me.

When I drove through the gates of M.S. Ramaiah Institute of Technology, Bangalore, the same sinking feeling visited me from back in 1984. The lump in my throat, the helplessness, and the choking, were all back – stronger this time. The gates of the institute resembled the wrought-iron black gates of the boarding school. Or perhaps my mind's eye chose to fashion the resemblance.

Papa accompanied me to settle me in at my new residence for four years. Even the taxi ride reminded me of the hour-long drive to my old boarding school. As I gazed out of the window, admiring how lush Bangalore looked in comparison to Delhi, his words echoed in my head. 'If you are unsure what you want to do, go for IT – computer science engineering,' he frequently said during my last year in school. 'It's a booming industry.' So, I found myself in Bangalore because of an Indianism: strive for nothing but the best academic grades and choose lucrative, highly respectable career paths such as engineering, medicine, or accountancy. I chose technology, purposely picking an institute hundreds of miles away from my extended family in Delhi.

Our taxi pulled up between two girls' hostels. The NRI (Non-Resident Indian) wing had spacious rooms with en-suites and a pantry. The annual rent for this was four times that of another girls' hostel opposite the NRI wing: four girls to a room and common bathrooms. Girls hanging around by the entrance of both hostels stared at us, watching us intently to see which hostel we would enter. Thank goodness Papa led the way to the NRI wing. I couldn't imagine sharing a room again. I felt the eyes of those from the other hostel on my back, and I smelt envy.

We whizzed through two days of furniture shopping, books and stationery purchases, and traversing the campus, familiarising myself with it all. All the while, the same few girls from the other hostel had their eyes on me.

Standing by the entrance of the hostel, his taxi waiting, Papa's parting words were, 'Ragging is a part of college life. Don't resist it and do what the girls say. I was ragged too. After a few weeks, seniors become your friends.'

'A few *weeks*?' I wasn't prepared to put up with bullying for another day. 'It's wrong! I'm not going to let anyone rag me.'

'Yes, it is wrong. Life is unfair. You will come across plenty of wrongs every day. You are now starting the next phase of your life where you will need to learn to differentiate between big wrongs and little wrongs. Often, you'll have to suck up the little wrongs. Big wrongs, stand up against them.' He placed his hand on my head, blessing me. We didn't hug. I can't remember if I ever hugged Papa after I entered adolescence.

I cried my way back to my room, cold and bland, covered from floor to ceiling in beige tiles. I had seen a few rooms, all as unwelcoming as each other. Pretty soon I wasn't sure if I was crying because I missed Papa already or because I loathed my room. Twenty minutes later, a knock at my door interrupted my sobbing. Two timid girls, in slippers and *salwar kameez*, hair oiled and plaited, said some senior girls had summoned me to their room. I had heard about the look freshers were meant to adopt. Its purpose was simple: to be easily identified as a fresher, susceptible to being ragged by any senior. I was going to be asked to dress the same for the entire first semester.

I followed the girls to the other hostel through a dingy corridor, walls so dirty, it was difficult to make out the original paint colour. Chatter from rooms on both sides echoed in the hallway. Some peered out from their rooms, curious to see the nervous freshers, sniggering and passing comments. I fought my nerves and walked with my head held high, ready to disobey every command.

'This one is going to be a troublemaker,' one said behind my back.

'More likely to get into trouble. She hasn't met Sanjana yet,' said another. Suddenly, the fear of this unknown senior covered my arms with goosebumps.

The two girls stopped at a door, almost at the end of the corridor, and left. Ragged already, their restlessness was evident. They couldn't wait to get away. Initially, they walked languidly and after a few metres, they scurried. I entered the seniors' den with caution, eyes pinned to the floor. The girls had told me on the way that under no circumstances was I to look up or make eye contact.

In my peripheral vision, I saw several pairs of feet. There must have been a dozen girls in the musty room, half the size of mine. The ones sitting down were seniors, and the ones standing in the line that I joined were freshers.

'Look, the NRI chick is here,' said one. 'Weren't you told to wear *salwar kameez* only for the first semester, not jeans and tight tops?'

'No ma'am.' I hadn't made a good start and was on their radar.

'Hands behind your back, like the others.'

'Yes ma'am.'

'Where are you from?'

'Japan, ma'am.'

'Aha, *Japani gudia*, Japanese doll,' said another voice, heavier, more authoritative. Later I learned it belonged to Sanjana.

'Girls, you have two options. Either you entertain us, or you do our chores.'

'What kind of chores, ma'am?' a voice spoke beside me.

'Wash our clothes, iron our clothes, dust and mop our rooms, and so on.'

The memory of washing Payal's clothes, for nearly two-and-a-half years in the boarding school, came rushing back. I grew restless, clenching my fists behind my back.

No brainer. Entertain them and get out.

'What's the matter, *chammak challo,* flashy girl? Stop dancing!' I didn't realise I was shuffling.

'Actually, will a dance be OK?' I asked.

'Oh yeah? Let's see what you got then, *chammak challo,*' Sanjana said. She instructed another girl to slip a cassette into the stereo system by the only window in the room, facing the corridor. I recognised the song straight away: *Made in India* by Alisha Chinai, the number-one hit released earlier that year.

As soon as I started dancing, Sanjana yelled, 'Eyes down!'

I lost my sense of balance several times with my head naturally falling with my eyes. It was the most torturous dance performance.

'You sure can dance,' she said when the song finished. 'You can entertain us every evening.'

'Yes ma'am.' It took a while to catch my breath and get my bearings again, the sweltering room making it harder to acclimatise. Meanwhile, the other girls in the queue offered to do chores instead.

'May I go now, ma'am?'

'You may.'

Phew! Put this down to a 'little wrong'. Dancing every day is all I have to do.

Relieved to have gotten away easily, I rushed to the door

when Sanjana's words, painfully familiar, stopped me.

'*Chammak challo*, who's that man who was here with you?'

I turned and stared at all the seniors huddled together.

'Eyes down! How many times do I have to tell you?'

I continued staring, now only at Sanjana. I will never know what she looked like because I saw Payal in her.

'He's my father!'

'Ha, can't be! If he's your father, mine is Amitabh Bachchan,' she scorned. "How's it possible for your father to be so fair and for you to be dark?"

Those were Payal's exact words ten years ago. The senior girls laughed because Sanjana did, and the freshers laughed like they were on a laughter cue. My arms behind my back, I clenched my fists so hard, my nails dug into the flesh of my palms, taking the brunt of my indignation.

This is a 'big wrong'. Stand up to it.

Once again, my audacity failed me. At that moment, I became the same six-year-old girl, standing in front of Payal, surrendering to her mocking. I felt weak without my parents, my pillars of strength. I asked again, 'Can I go now, ma'am?'

Sanjana flicked her right hand, signalling her permission. I was out the door when I heard her say, 'Think I hit a raw nerve. Let the games begin.'

That night, as I fretted over what games Sanjana would play, I was kept awake by the realisation that my colour was the 'biggest wrong' of my life. It let me down daily. If there was any 'B' I desperately wanted in my life, it was Belonging. I wanted to belong to my parents, and I wanted people to believe that I did.

In the morning, dressed in a white *salwar kameez*, flip flops, and hair tied back as instructed, I headed to the strip of local shops outside the campus in search of a solution. Across the road from the main gate stood a humongous billboard advertising a South Indian movie. It featured a very fair actress alongside a relatively dark-skinned actor. Given that South Indians tended to be darker than North Indians on average, the obsession with fairness here was even more disconcerting. Or even more justified, depending on your view. Here too, it was common for their actresses to be fair-skinned, and the actors duskier. Despite all the differences between North and South India – the food, culture, festivals, and attire – there was one unifying factor: the existence of colourism.

Next to the billboard, in a corner shop, I caught a glimpse of the whitening cream. It sat there, seducing me. During the many summer holidays in India, I frequently encountered the cream. I lusted after it, stealing furtive glances as if at an ex-boyfriend, but too afraid to start the relationship again. Too afraid of being caught, of not doing it right.

Now, I had the freedom to fix my colour without inhibition. I couldn't resist the temptation; the cream teased me with its presence, placed intentionally on shelves at the front end of the store. I yielded to the thrill of cheating.

The shop was quiet, unlike the previous few times I had visited for small household items when students loitered around. The shelves were packed to the brim, every item squeezed in as though picking one out would send the shop's entire stock tumbling like domino pieces. Shoppers didn't have the luxury of walking through aisles, picking up required items, and adding them to their baskets. Everything to be bought was behind the shopkeeper, who had developed a skill of swiftly but carefully plucking out items. All you could do was point to what you wanted, ask for it, and he would keep things aside for you on his table. The shopkeeper was a young man, a college student, with a thick, jet-black moustache that ended where his lips ended, and he wore the brightest T-shirts, always with stonewashed blue jeans. His hair was always oiled and gave off a strong scent of jasmine. Unlike his counterpart, in Delhi, this man was uninterested in small talk.

By the time I crossed the road and reached the shop, a few students had congregated, mostly men. I hesitated at first. *What if they see me buying the cream and snigger? What if one of them is the next Wicked Man? What if they tease me like The Boys?* I wasn't considered dark in Bangalore, though. I was one of the fairer ones here. I wouldn't have to face any tormenting remarks. How I wish I had walked away then, realising this. At last, I was in a land where I could just *be*. But Sanjana's words were the last punch. Knockout. I surrendered.

'What do you need? Others are waiting behind you,' said the shopkeeper, his tone curt.

'Can I have that cream?' I muttered under my breath.

'What?'

'That cream,' I said, pointing to a popular one.

He plucked it out from the top shelf and placed it on the table.

'Anything else?' he asked, tapping on the table with his forefinger. I waited for the loitering students, expecting a reaction. Nothing. Nothing at all. They continued chatting as if I wasn't even there. I slipped the cream into the black handbag slung across my shoulder.

'Nothing else, thank you.'

The third person in the queue, a lady, asked for the cream too, unabashedly. My affair with the cream didn't need to be clandestine after all. A sense of liberation came over me, giving me wings to practically fly back to the room, wearing a grin from ear to ear.

When I discovered the cream's consistency was still thick and didn't spread evenly, I wet my hands to moisten my palms. A few water drops helped spread it. Instant result. There was a white glow and a minute change in colour, just like dabbing on talcum powder. It did what it said on the tube.

From then on, the cream became a standard item on my dressing table. Like a cigarette to a smoker or drugs to an addict, it was my 'little wrong'. I could see my colour 'improving', my confidence improving, and the joy it brought me was far greater than worrying about doing the right thing. It became my drug. Or to put it mildly, a household item on the shopping list: toothpaste, shampoo, sanitary pads, and fairness cream.

I became addicted to it, liberated on the surface, enslaved on the inside. Sanjana pushed my buttons a few more times, repeatedly insinuating that I may not be my father's daughter. I ignored it and danced with fierce confidence, feeling more beautiful as the cream worked its magic. She stopped ragging me only a few days in.

I put down catcalling to the cream's magic too, cherishing the attention of several boys. Deepak, a senior, started visiting the hostel frequently. At first, I thought he visited to rag me. Bulging biceps and broad shoulders, his sporty physique, incredibly irresistible on his motorbike, was a magnet for many girls. Each time he called for me, I would reluctantly meet him, hiding my usual chatty self behind the pretence of a timid girl, dressed in a salwar kameez, eyes down. He only received one-word answers from me, for a maximum of ten minutes, before I started fidgeting, asking to go. He still turned up every day.

'Don't you realise he's into you?' said Anisha, standing at the door of her room opposite mine. Deepak and she were classmates. She was a senior, but I hardly saw her dressed in anything other than a *salwar kameez*. Fair, with jet-black hair, she kept a low profile.

'You're crazy,' I said in disbelief. I also pretended not to be interested in him.

'Trust me, a girl like Sanjana wouldn't let you get away this easily. She's backed off because he must have told her to.'

The next day, I introduced my real self to Deepak. I wore black jeans and a baby pink top, my long, wavy hair swaying above my waist.

'Coffee?' he said, surprised that I was still talking to him after an hour. With eye contact. We sat on his motorbike. As I imagined wrapping my arms around his washboard abs, a tingling electric current ran through my body.

It must be the cream. I've just bagged a boyfriend. Not just any boyfriend, a hunky boyfriend with light brown eyes and a delicious shy-guy charm.

Deepak and I dated for two years. We hung out, carefree, all over Bangalore and never missed the latest Bollywood movie screening in cinemas. Around this time in the late nineties, Bollywood started featuring white background dancers behind the lead actor or actress. This formula proved to be an instant hit, attracting a larger audience to the cinemas. White dancers danced more erotically, often seen gyrating against the lead, and of course, they were seen as more exotic because of their colour. But there was also a new dusky Bollywood actress, Kajol, who rose to fame from the movie *Dilwale Dulhania Le Jayenge*. After its release in October 1995, Deepak and I watched it at least five times in the cinemas. Kajol went on to become an A-list star in Bollywood. Again, I grew hopeful that change was in the air as a few more 'less than fair' actresses entered Bollywood and appeared to be accepted by the general public.

After Deepak left to pursue a master's degree in the US, I stopped going to the cinema. I missed him and couldn't bear to sit through romantic movies. We kept in touch, declaring our eternal love for each other, and even talked about getting married in the future. Despite daily emails from internet cafes, international calls once a week from an ISTD phone booth, and mailing photos with kisses, the fate of our relationship was no different to most long-distance relationships: it withered and eventually died.

My relationship with the cream was stronger than ever, though. Unlike my unabashed displays of affection towards Deepak, no one knew about the cream. No one was a party to this secret.

25

A SUITABLE BOY

August 1999, Japan

Even being in a marital relationship (in which one shouldn't have any secrets) didn't guilt me into sharing mine.

Having just returned home after a four-year engineering degree, the last thing on my mind was to meet someone. I hadn't applied for jobs during campus recruitment, hadn't given my future any thought, apart from possibly applying for a master's degree. Only after I got my fix of family time.

'Shall we head to London this December, for the millennium celebrations?' Papa asked, holding an envelope in his hand.

'Is this a trick question?' I replied. I was craving a family vacation. Then I noticed Papa's cheeky smile. 'What's that you're holding?'

'There's a family in London who...' Papa said. I should have known there was a hidden agenda.

'No way! Don't even think about it. I've just come back!'

'Just take a look at this picture. You know us, *beta*. The decision will be entirely yours.'

I wasn't against introductory marriages. To be honest, I didn't know any different because no one on either side of my family had had a love marriage. Papa knew about Deepak and went to meet him in Boston. A fruitless trip, considering that we broke up months later.

'I can't. I'm not even thinking about it, Papa.'

As he flashed a photograph at me, I turned towards my room – *my* room. When I was in Bangalore, my family had moved to a three-bedroom apartment in a prestigious building above the Indian Social Society Club. I finally had a room I could call mine, a room that could host my secret, daily. The cream, after four years of use, had certainly 'improved' my colour. Mummy noticed it at the airport when picking me up. 'Your colour is *saaf*, clean, now,' she effused. Such remarks had once bothered me. After I surrendered to the Fairometer, they fell on deaf ears.

'Think about it, Shweta. Such *rishtas* don't come around daily,' Papa said.

Rishtas. In the four years when I was in Bangalore, one of the summer breaks was cut short as exams were delayed. Because I couldn't make it to Japan, the family came to Delhi instead. One conversation in Karol Bagh between Papa and a distant uncle remains fresh in my mind. Papa happened to ask this uncle if he knew of any good suitors for me.

'How much will you spend on the wedding?' asked the uncle, his unsubtle glance at me saying more than his words.

'If that's how you start conversations about potential matches, we're done,' scorned Papa.

Thankfully, this *rishta* in London wasn't suggested by that uncle. 'All right. Just one meeting. No pressure. And absolutely no cheesy tea-and-samosas meeting,' I said, standing in my bedroom doorway.

'We've already bought you a sari for that meeting. You don't have the make the samosas. We can buy them from the shops,' Papa chuckled.

'Very funny.'

Neeraj, of course, jumped with joy about the potential holiday. 'We'll have fun for sure,' I winked at him. Our relationship had become more amicable over the years. Either he had matured, or I had become less jealous of him. His curls had transformed into a spiky hairstyle. His lashes were still the envy of every girl, his skin tone still a mix of our parents' fair complexion. But he never compared his colour with mine, not even during one of our many fights. Perhaps he subconsciously remembered my sisterly love for him when he used to sleepwalk, exposed and vulnerable. Perhaps he knew my colour was my biggest weakness.

I asked Papa to pass me the photo of my marriage suitor. Beaming, he slipped it into my hands.

'What's his name?' I asked, glancing at the photograph.

'Amit.'

My instinctive reaction was, 'Nah, looks too serious.'

The thought of visiting London thrilled me. In our childhood days, Kanika and I used to spend hours on Sundays in two foreign mansions, only a few minutes down the road from my building. These mansions, small museums really, were known as *Ijinkans*. They were a portal to a mesmerizing, foreign world: floral wallpaper, dainty tea sets, patterned upholstery, rosewood furniture, and ornate wall decorations.

Our apartment looked lacklustre in comparison. There was a trunk of accessories somewhere in the two houses. At the end of the visit, we would adorn ourselves with pearl necklaces and posh hats, pretending to be The Queen of England. The thought that I might one day visit England never crossed my mind. Life really does drop lots of hints about your future if you've got an eye for them.

We arrived in London on a chilly evening in late December of 1999, checking in to a weekly apartment in Mayfair, off Park Lane. Moseying down Oxford Street, I noticed people from all backgrounds and ethnicities dressed mostly in black. Black trousers, black tops, black dresses, black overcoats, black umbrellas. Christmas lights brought a dash of colour to the street, like fireflies in the dark. I had worn a black top only once. '*Kala* colour, *kale* clothes, and unruly hair, what are you trying to do? Look like a witch?' Maya Mami had said. After that, I only bought my first black outfit, a sari, when I was in Bangalore, away from her critical eyes and when my colour had lightened.

The next day, at the entrance of La Porte des Indes, a fusion Indian and Portuguese restaurant off Marble Arch, I quivered from the fear of rejection. Never mind whether Amit was a suitable boy for me. Was I a suitable girl for him? From my teenage years, I had been told that this was the ultimate purpose of every Indian woman of marriageable age: to meet a suitable husband. No doubt I had grown several shades lighter, a caramel colour, after using the cream for a few years and staying out of the sun in Bangalore. After Deepak left, my daily routine included attending classes and a visit to the canteen and the library. Occasionally, I would go out with friends in the evening. But I was still nowhere near as fair as my parents. If I had met Amit on my own – without them – I was confident I would not be rejected. During the four years spent in Bangalore, I had gotten plenty of attention from boys. Although I wasn't going to say yes anyway, I feared rejection from this family; I couldn't bear to be the cause of embarrassment to my parents.

I grew anxious, shuffling from side to side in my chalk-grey *salwar kameez*. 'Only light colours suit dark skin,' Maya Mami used to say.

From the corner of my eyes, I saw a young man, dressed in all black, pacing up and down on the mezzanine floor, a few steps down from reception. While he was engrossed in a serious conversation on his mobile phone, I was drawn to his deep and incredibly attractive voice. He didn't notice that I couldn't take my eyes off him.

I wish I was meeting him.

'Come on, the table is downstairs,' said Papa, buttoning up the blazer of his grey suit. A so-called quick, informal lunch in formal wear.

'Just lunch and nothing more, OK?' I whispered to Papa. Neeraj and Mummy were ahead of us, a few steps down. When I turned to the mezzanine floor, the young man was gone.

I started making my way down the white marble steps, catching up with Mummy. In all these years, she hadn't aged a day. Dressed in a peacock-green sari and simple make-up – just her favourite maroon lipstick – I watched her gracefully totter down the steps.

You will never be as beautiful as Mummy and as fair as Papa. Brace yourself for all the judging. This is only the first family introduction.

My breathing grew heavier. I held on to the banister harder. Just a few more steps and we would be on the ground floor, heading to our table. Then, out of the blue, the same young man I had seen earlier appeared at the bottom of the staircase. Next to him was an Indian lady dressed in a magenta sari and a gold choker necklace.

'Hi, I'm Amit,' he smiled. His light brown eyes sparkled. 'This is my mum.'

Have you ever met someone whose charm swept you off your feet from their first spoken words? That was what happened to me that afternoon. Amit's photo failed to capture his charm or his looks.

'You should fire your photographer,' I wanted to tell him. What I actually said was a plain and simple, 'Hi.'

We walked past several palm trees and multiple sections of the enormous restaurant, its walls painted a warm yellow shade. Seven of us sat in a private section, chatting for hours as though the families knew each other. In a way, we did know each other. Bade Papa and Amit's uncle lived in the same building in Singapore. Friends and business associates, they played cupid, scheming for us to meet, believing that we were a perfect match for each other.

Amit's eyes did not leave my face. No snarky comments about colour were made by his family. I attributed that to the cream. I didn't give him or his parents any credit for not being colourists. Shame I didn't give *myself* credit either for the person that I was. Because my colour had been everyone's concern all my life, by now, it had become mine too. I had seen undue importance being given to colour, masking flaws *and* virtues.

Amit and I talked endlessly. At around 5 p.m., both sets

of parents said, 'Why don't you kids carry on? Feel free to go out for the evening.'

When I told Mummy I'd need to get a change of clothes from the hotel first, Mummy said she had already packed my black jeans and a jumper in a bag. She had clearly planned for this meeting to be more than just a quick lunch, and I was glad she had.

Leaving the restaurant, a bitterly cold gust of wind hit us. 'I hear investment banking is a tough industry. Long working hours?' I asked Amit, rubbing my hands, almost wanting to hold his hand.

'Yes,' he said. 'I have just finished working on a big merger. Luckily, I've got the whole week off now.'

'Luckily,' I said, flirting. The first time I had the confidence to flirt. We met every night after that. And every night, I returned to the apartment later than the previous night. Besotted with each other, we got engaged on the last day of the holiday and decided to tie the knot seven months later in July 2000 in Delhi.

In the months before the wedding, I went through a rigorous beauty regime, staying indoors, applying homemade skin-lightening body scrubs, and of course the all-important fairness creams, day and night. I even opted for full-body bleaching in the bridal makeover package at a five-star hotel in Delhi. While the beautician looking after me for the day was preparing the room, I sat waiting in nothing but a white robe given to me by the beauty salon.

'Ma'am, a head massage is included in the bridal package,' said a stout, short man with a moustache. Before

I had the chance to acknowledge him, he started running his fingers through my hair. His sinister smile and invasion of my personal space reminded me of The Creepy Man. But I nodded and let him do his work. I relaxed my shoulders and nestled into the chair. As he started massaging my neck, with perfect pressure but rough hands, I wondered why a masseuse's hands weren't softer. A few minutes later, his hands moved down to my shoulders. He pulled my robe down slightly; it sat on the shoulder bones. While he worked on the knots, I dozed off, my head dropping forward in slow motion. Moments later, I jumped straight up. I turned around to scan the room, but the masseuse had vanished after slipping his hand under my robe and groping me.

I had never imagined that I would be groped in a public, professional place, a beauty salon in a five-star hotel. Feeling violated by the assault, I was shaking with anger. And hot like I had spiked a temperature.

Just then, my beautician called me in. I should have asked her about this man. I should have seen him punished. As I lay on the treatment bed, watching her apply bleach all over my body, I replayed what had happened in my head.

Who will believe me? How would I prove it?

I told myself that it didn't happen. I must have imagined it. Or dreamed it. It must have been The Creepy Man's presence in my subconscious, playing games with me. But the touch felt real. I shuddered in abhorrence at the thought. As I oscillated between the two scenarios – dream versus reality – the tingling from the bleach and the pungent smell started to distract me. A few seconds in and the tingling was so strong, my focus shifted from what had happened to wanting to scratch my entire body. I had always wondered about the effect of strong chemicals on the skin, but because several beauticians in Bangalore had suggested bleaching twice a month for fairer skin, I killed my curiosity. I bleached regularly for 4 years. If only I had taken the time to understand the harmful effects of long-term use.

Even after the whole bleaching regime, I was deemed 'not fair enough' by my wedding make-up artist. I was furious when she started smearing on a foundation a few shades lighter than my actual tone. I was about to ask her for a foundation that matched my skin, but what about what I had been doing to my natural colour for years? The realisation of this blatant hypocrisy stopped me. Browsing through our wedding photos days later, the ghostlike make-up bothered me. I had surrendered to colourism and although remnants of a fight resurfaced occasionally, for vanity, I suppressed them.

26

B FOR BRAZILIAN

September 2000, England

'Hey, love, where are you from?' said a good-looking English man in a pub. He had blue eyes and dark hair.

It was a Friday, around 3 p.m. when I caught a bus from King's College in the city to Paddington. I had enrolled in a master's degree in computer science, unclear why because it never interested me. Often, when we're good at something, we convince ourselves that we enjoy it too. My first-class degree from Bangalore had deluded me into believing I was finally enjoying the subject. In reality, I was enjoying the experience of being a student in London and making new friends at the college.

Cotton candy clouds were scattered across a clear blue sky. A mild September breeze ruffled through my wavy hair. English summers weren't anything like Indian summers; they were damp and rainy most of the time. Unlike in India, I had started to appreciate the rare appearance of the sun. I finished my classes early that day and headed to Paddington to look for an apartment.

As usual, Amit was running late, stuck on a conference call. I had lined up quite a few apartment viewings in Paddington. Waiting for Amit to join, I sat by the bar area in The Swan pub, opposite the station. Groups of young people were trickling in, taking advantage of happy hour, which started at 4 p.m.

'Are you Brazilian, love?' said the English man, taking a sip from his pint of Guinness, shifting closer to me.

'I'm Indian,' I replied, quickly turning my back to the man.

'You've got a Brazilian look, love,' he said.

Whatever he meant by 'a Brazilian look', two things were obvious - that it was a compliment and that he was trying to flirt with me.

After all the negative nicknames with a 'B' – Bedwetter, Blackie, Bastard – 'Brazilian' was the first compliment. Over the years, I received many more compliments.

'I love your colour.'

'Such an exotic colour. I struggle to look like that after several beach holidays.'

'I need to go to a tanning salon to look like you. Even then my colour looks artificial. You are very lucky.'

All of these were, of course, said by English classmates, friends, and colleagues. Never Indian. My extended family's contrary observations during every Skype call were: 'Your colour has improved' or 'Looks like London suits you.' Of course, it suited me. When your skin is deprived of sunshine, naturally you will grow paler. But I wasn't complaining. While almost every conversation in London began with discussing the miserable weather, I only saw fair weather.

I can't deny it: the compliments from my family were far more intoxicating. After all, isn't that what we all yearn for? Compliments from strangers don't come close to praise from family. But intoxication and pressure are a lethal combination, like a friend at a pub asking you to down one more drink.

'Have you met Mrs Khanna's daughter-in-law? She is so beautiful and fair,' extolled Mrs Patil at a dinner party, as she helped my mother-in-law and me clear up the table. Mrs Patil reminded me of an Indian soap opera actress, playing the role of a dramatic, tactless aunty. Her yellow sari was so bright, my eyes begged for a break. I excused myself from the table and headed to the kitchen to load the dishwasher.

'Thank your lucky stars Amit chose you, Shweta,' she said, following me, narrowing her eyes slightly. 'He fell for your bubbly personality. Amit had many beautiful girls in line wanting to marry him.'

I understood her motive and decided that responding wasn't worth it.

'Mrs. Patil, shall we lay the dessert on the table?' my mother-in-law interjected. After Mrs Patil left, Amit's mother told me that Mrs Patil had her eyes on Amit for her daughter – fair, of course. She thought her daughter deserved Amit more than I did.

The pressure to remain fair didn't end after getting married. All my life, it had been drummed into me, both subliminally and explicitly, that the penultimate phase – getting married – should be the sole goal in life for a woman. I say 'penultimate' because post-marriage is the ultimate phase. Two phrases that were said more often than I would have liked to hear were:

'*Shaadi kaise hogi*, how will you get married?' Because of my colour.

'Do what you like *shaadi ke baad*, after you're married.' Because of my gender.

Apparently, marriage was the ticket to freedom; to wearing what you wanted – I wore bikinis, halter necks, miniskirts; to having a career if you wanted – I started working at UBS Investment Banking's IT department; to being yourself – I started running a Bollywood dance company. All subject to the implicit approval of my new family, of course. Not when it came to colour. I felt the pressure for the first two decades of my life to be a 'fair and beautiful' daughter. And after marriage, to be a 'fair and beautiful' daughter-in-law, thanks to aunties like Mrs Patil. Hers wasn't the only taunt I heard over the next few years.

I often used to argue about my identity being so much more than that of a daughter and a daughter-in-law. I did find freedom in the ultimate post-wedding phase. Amit and his parents were modern and broad-minded. How I wish I could find freedom from the claws of colourism. I couldn't part ways with the cream and wavered between the intoxication of compliments and societal pressure to stay light-skinned.

By 2004, I had become much fairer. Overconfidence persuaded me to board a flight to Thailand for our first beach holiday. With my newfound confidence, through my new skin tone, I enjoyed showing off tan lines, as western holidaymakers do. That joy didn't last long. I received many disheartening comments on Skype calls with extended family after returning with a tan.

Back to the cream.

27

BELONGING

September 2009, Japan

As a young couple, Amit and I had travelled a fair amount, 'preferring' hectic city breaks to leisurely beach holidays – barring Thailand. Well, Amit was always keen on beach holidays, but I came up with ample excuses to avoid them. Sometimes, he would pick up on my insecurities when I would complain about even the slightest tan from enjoying a rare, glorious day in London. Despite Amit being the most important person in my life, his reassurance that colour meant nothing to him was meaningless to me. Validation from the greater community is what I always sought.

Post-marriage wasn't the penultimate episode in this series after all. Just when you think your series is going to end, your life announces a surprise episode with a new character - a child. When I was expecting Kareena in 2006, I didn't bother to have colour 'enhancing' food and drinks, like milk with a pinch of saffron. Yet when she was born, the first thought that went through my mind was, 'Thank God she's fair.' I didn't want her to go through what I had. Then, when I brought her home, I promised myself that I would never project my insecurities onto her, allowing my little girl to freely enjoy the sun. I never let colourism get anywhere near her, yet it never left me. Rohan's birth in 2008 didn't have me fretting over his colour. I had questioned sexism in colourism decades ago. Now I was perpetuating it subconsciously.

While I was celebrating life with my two beautiful children, 2009 arrived with devastating news: Papa had terminal cancer and his health had deteriorated; the same kidney cancer that took Baba's life in 1994. I had forgiven Baba and was sad to see him go. But decades later, I am still trying to forgive his cancer genes. Papa's cancer had spread from the lymph nodes in his kidneys to his lungs. Knowing that he had limited time, he wanted to see Neeraj, now 27, married. Kobe saw its first grand Indian wedding in the most luxurious hotel in the city, the Ana Crowne Plaza, offering serene views of the city and of Rokko Mountain.

Moving from Jaipur, a small city in India to Japan must have been overwhelming for Arpita, Neeraj's wife. But she didn't show it. Arpita, hazel-eyed and fair-skinned, went about adjusting discreetly even to her dying and often agitated (because of pain) father-in-law. Papa's health declined rapidly after the wedding. On my fourth and last trip to Japan in September 2009, I found myself praying on an aeroplane once again.

Please don't depart for heaven until I see you, Papa. Hang in there.

After I landed, and during every moment in the car ride from Kansai Airport to the hospital, Daigaku Byoin, I prayed and prayed. When I entered Papa's room on the eighth floor,

I was relieved to see him alive. For once, the Almighty had listened to my prayers.

'*Beta*!' he said, with all the energy he could muster. His voice had become coarse, a side effect of all the medication, I was told. His favourite light-blue striped pyjamas hung on his frail body as if he was a hanger. His double chin sagged low, covering the top of his neck. Papa, now bald, with a cannula in his right hand, dragged his body up to a sitting position.

'Papa,' I held his other hand in mine, holding back my tears. 'I want you to know you are my hero.'

'*Beta*, I feel . . .'

'You can do this, Papa. You are my hero and I know you can.' I knew he was on his deathbed, so I am not sure what I expected him to be able to do – fight imminent death? I wanted to say so much more. I wanted to thank him for his sacrifices and for the life he had given me, but Rohan, a year old, was wailing in Mummy's arms. With visible dark circles and an enervated body from countless hospital trips, she still tried to pacify my son. I could tell Mummy had been crying all night too. I took Rohan out of the room and never got a chance to return. Neeraj drove us home in our family's new car, a BMW, number plate 1214, Neeraj's birthday. In the car, I reflected on how robbed I felt of my time with Papa. Away in boarding school, then college, then married less than a year after returning. I regretted every time I spoke to him rudely. I cherished all his cheesy jokes. His hearty laugh rang in my ears. Driving past Nishimura Coffee, a broken clock on the other side of the road – with its hands stuck at 5.46 a.m. – reminded me of the earthquake fourteen years ago. A reminder of our family's survival and all that Papa and Mummy had done to ensure we were safe. A reminder, also, of the city's revival.

Fourteen years later, Kobe had revived. Papa had not.

The next morning at around 7 a.m., when I was on the way to the hospital with one of our family friends, we received the news. Papa had passed. He was 56. He took his last breath in Neeraj's arms. No words can describe the pain, the void. That night, I slept with his mobile phone by my side; Papa and his phone were inseparable. Tears flowed freely, as did visitors with condolences.

A day later, we held prayers in a crematorium hall with Papa resting in his coffin at the back. A couple of months before, the Indian community in Kobe had gathered to celebrate a joyous occasion, Neeraj's wedding, with us. Now the same people gathered in sympathy. Among The Boys, Angad was the first to call and then visit. That day, I saw a different Angad approaching me. His thick glasses had been replaced by contact lenses. His short legs had caught up with his long strides. He was six-feet-two-inches tall. I had, of course, witnessed these changes in the last couple of decades as we transitioned from adolescence to adulthood, just as I had witnessed our growing friendship. Every time I visited Kobe from Bangalore, The Boys and The Girls would meet up for dinner. At my bachelorette party, I invited the entire group; everything was twice as much fun with The Boys. The night before I left Kobe for good, I threw another impromptu party at home. Playing truth or dare, Angad dared to wear one of my skirts. For the rest of the night, he sat in the living room amongst us all wearing my skirt, drinking rum and Coke and laughing the night away. At some point, he even helped me pack my four suitcases. After we both got married and every time I visited Kobe, we would meet for dinner with our respective spouses. The Angad today, with compassionate and sympathetic eyes, was whom I wanted Papa to meet, unlike the only other time they had interacted on the staircase of The India Club. I wanted to tell Papa, 'He *is* a good boy.'

That evening, one of Papa's old college friends visited us at home. I had never met him. He happened to have started teaching at Kobe University as a professor. I can't remember the subject. He looked a lot older than Papa, his unruly salt-and-pepper hair in desperate need of a cut. His moustache could have done with a trim too; I could barely see his upper lip when he spoke the words I had yearned for all my life, 'You look just like your father.'

At last, I belong!

I sobbed in my room. These words should have been the catalyst for change in me. After all, wanting to look like Papa was the main reason to reach for the cream. I still don't know why I didn't stop then. Perhaps because Papa was no more.

Two days later, we travelled to Delhi with Papa's ashes. Amit and Kareena flew to Delhi from London. During the remaining twelve days of mourning, more guests visited freely, day and night. Every morning, two pundits started the day with prayers sitting cross-legged on the floor. In front of them lay a small fire pit, herbs, and some food items. They performed a *havan*, a fire ritual, for Papa's soul to leave peacefully. Mummy, Neeraj, Arpita, the newlywed addition to our family, and Bade Papa contributed to his peaceful departure by partaking in the *havan*.

When I stepped forward to participate, one pundit abruptly put his hand out. 'You don't have to join,' he said.

Sleeves folded up, his unusually hairy forearm stretched above the flames of the *havan*. Unlike all the pundits I had met in the past, he was young and slim.

'Why not?'

'Because you don't belong to the family anymore.'

'I am his daughter. What do you mean I don't belong?'

'Yes, but you're married. After *kanyadaan,* giving away the bride in the presence of the holy fire, daughters don't belong to their families.'

'I don't belong although he brought me into this world and cared for me for decades? And my sister-in-law, only married for two months, is now more of a part of my family than I am?' I asked, shaking.

Arpita became visibly uncomfortable. I apologised to her. She understood this wasn't about her. Holding my hand gently, she looked the pundit in the eye. 'Didi *will* be a part of these prayers,' she commanded firmly in her soft voice. Arpita didn't wait for Bade Papa's permission. Nor did she care about what others in the family would think. Her understated tenacity won me over.

As I was about to offer a pinch of herbs into the *havan*, the pundit, a Brahmin scholar, itched to have the last word.

'You can do it. But your participation won't make a difference. It won't reach your father's soul,' he said.

'This is bullshit!' I exclaimed. 'Papa has given me the life I have and you're telling me I can't give back in any way to his departing soul?'

What will it take to belong?

I heard Arpita calling for me when I was storming out the front door, but I didn't turn around. Already angry with the Almighty for taking Papa away too soon, I grew even more furious at traditional Hindu religious practices after that. I stopped believing in any such practices and deliberately defied them. Hypocritical cultural norms, patriarchal practices such as the fast of *karva chauth* for your husband's long life, which men did not reciprocate for their wives, and rules around periods, I challenged them all. Except for colourism, which had become my blind spot. Perhaps because my addiction had pulled me too deep into the dark abyss of skin-whitening products.

Over a year later, the family moved to India. Japan didn't feel like home without Papa. Meanwhile, I continued to line the pockets of the manufacturers of fairness creams. With two young children to entertain, we swapped exploring bustling cities for the sand, sea, and indulgence of cocktails by the poolside. The exchange cost me a demotion on the Fairometer. I sacrificed my vanity for the happiness of my children, splashed for hours in the pool until our fingertips turned to prunes, slurped on slushies, and snuggled on sunbeds as they dozed off. I also watched them turn several shades darker. Every holiday, we would compare tan lines. It was a fun game for them. Not for me. I had my own game to play and had taught myself to enjoy it. I had been playing the game of the high striker, seen in fairgrounds, with my personal Fairometer. The amount of effort and time required for my skincare routine was tiresome. I'd strike first with the creams, then strike harder – staying out of the sun and wearing hats – all for the puck to fly up marginally higher. Then I would see it plunge dramatically after just one beach holiday. One step forward, two steps back. The tan from multiple holidays in the sun resulted in a gradual change in skin tone. Irreversible. Regardless, I had blind faith in the cream. Like an educated fool. I lived my 'little wrong' for so long, I had forgotten why it felt wrong in the first place.

28
'THE BIG WRONG'
2016 to 2022

By now you've probably gathered I'm good at keeping secrets. Hiding the cream from Amit didn't take much effort compared to the other secrets I had buried for so long. However, it wasn't child's play hiding it from a child.

In 2016, by the poolside in Koh Samui, after Kareena caught me in possession of the cream, I didn't take the invasion of privacy well. I also expected her to understand. Having shared my entire life story with her, the majority of which even Amit was unaware of, I eagerly waited for her reaction. The sun had shifted its position slightly and so had I, protecting my body under the shade of the umbrella. I hadn't taken a sip of my piña colada; condensation from the glass created a ring of water around it. As I watched her finish the last bit of her second chocolate ice cream, I felt as nervous and exposed as one does on stage after a long monologue.

'Mummy, there have been some really mean people in your life who've made you feel this way,' said Kareena. 'But you have to stop using the cream. You always tell us that everyone is beautiful as they are.'

For a moment, I thought, *That's it? You have nothing else to say?* Then I realised I wasn't sure what else I expected from her anyway. She was only nine. And children are usually tough audiences. To her, there was no cloud of confusion, the cloud that loomed over my head for decades. I barely received any sympathy. She had adopted my style of tough love. I never thought that would catapult back to me.

'I want you to promise me…a *Mummy's Promise*,' she demanded.

Now she had me. I didn't use to promise the children much but when I did, I would say 'It's a Mummy's Promise', which to them was as good as written in stone. I always delivered a Mummy's Promise.

Her simple yet powerful message hit home, filling me with guilt, but it did not hit the bullseye. I wasn't ready to give up my vanity just yet. Even before we shook hands, I knew I was making a false promise, to her and to myself. How could I break a twenty-one-year-old relationship with the cream? Go cold turkey? Not a chance. Besides, my 'little wrong' wasn't causing anyone else any harm. I convinced her that I would reform.

Another big drop in my vessel of tolerance was a flying visit to Delhi in October 2019 for a cousin's wedding. I hadn't visited India in three years and for some odd reason, I expected lots of change. The Creepy Man hadn't changed. I still felt his eyes on me the entire time I was on the dance floor at the wedding. There was no change in attitudes towards colourism either. Or so I thought.

Spa treatments in India are irresistible. There are several salons and spa clubs in a parade of shops opposite Mummy's apartment building. If I'm honest, apart from seeing family, these treatments are always next on my priority list; I book them within hours of landing. There is an antiquated salon that I always visit. It doesn't have a printed treatment menu, operates on a cash-only policy, and the staff changes frequently. Nostalgia still draws me there.

'Which facial would you like, ma'am?'

I didn't recognise the lady assigned to me for my treatments. Preparing myself for pampering, I wriggled on the massage table. Eyes closed, arms tucked in, I exhaled and waited for her to spoil me with choices, running through each one verbally.

'We have a great skin-whitening facial,' she said, oblivious that she had pressed on my rawest nerve.

'Why? Do you think I need a skin-whitening facial?'

'No, ma'am,' she stuttered. 'I meant a tan-removing facial.'

Now she was not only pressing the nerve but stabbing it too.

'Do we know each other? Have we met before?'

'No, ma'am.'

'Then how do you know that I am tanned, and this is not my natural colour?'

'Sorry, ma'am. I asked as this is our most popular facial, to look fairer.'

Seething, I counted to ten. She wasn't at fault. She was simply offering the most popular choice. I asked for a fruit facial and let her get on with her business. When she finished, I asked if I could get my legs and arms waxed too as the salon didn't seem busy. She nodded, turned the wax heating pot on, and brought me some magazines. Flipping through them, I noticed many dusky Bollywood stars from the late '90s appeared significantly lighter by 2019.

I stepped out of the treatment room, keen to complain to the salon owner that such facials only fuel colourism.

It's pointless. Antiquated salon, antiquated mentality. Of course, salons would offer skin-whitening facials if Bollywood celebrities were advocating skin-whitening.

Outside the salon, I saw a few youngsters in their twenties, arguing by a parked red car. I had the urge to read the number plate - old habits die hard – but the group was obstructing my view. Two men, wanting to stay clear of the argument, sat in the car whilst the two ladies continued quarrelling. Waiting to cross the road, I caught snippets of their dispute. 'I don't want my shoulder and arm turning *kala*,' said one, insisting on sitting on the shady side of the car for the journey back. As tempted as I was to see the argument resolved, I knew it could go on for a while. Besides, standing on a dusty road, air pollution practically visible to the naked eye, I didn't want to negate the effect of the facial.

When I reached our apartment on the eighth floor, a wall of aromas greeted me. My mouth was watering, ready to devour my mother's homemade food. I sat at the dining table, famished, and switched on the television to distract myself. Browsing through channels, an advertisement for a fairness cream caught my attention. Over the last two decades, my annual summer holiday trips to India had reduced to infrequent flying visits. During those visits, I hadn't paid much attention to the numerous advertisements featuring A-list Bollywood actresses. They usually targeted women, convincing them that fairer skin will attract more men. I discovered that some creams were now selling to the burgeoning male market. This advertisement, though, targeted modern Indian women with career aspirations. Its message: gain self-confidence by feeling beautiful and win that job.

Unbelievable!

Decades ago, this cream had millions of women believe that they couldn't conquer the beauty world because of their dark skin. Now it had them believe they wouldn't get their desired job without it either. The colourism narrative had widened from 'fair is beautiful' to 'fair is successful'! Riled up after seeing that advertisement, I didn't notice my five-year-old niece running toward me until she jumped onto my lap. 'You have hair like spaghetti. I like your hair,' she said, twirling my curls in her fingers.

'Thank you, my darling, and I like your hair,' I chuckled, returning the compliment. She continued to play with my hair.

'Shweta Bua,' she said, resting her soft, chubby arm on mine. 'Why is your skin *kala*?'

A five-year-old had already been introduced to the world of colourism. An innocent five-year-old had managed to offend me. Children say what pops into their minds, but I did wonder why other differences between us didn't intrigue her, such as the difference between my dark brown and her grey-green eyes or the difference between our hair, black and curly versus straight and light brown.

Why colour? Was I overthinking this? Her observation wasn't, 'Why is your colour different to mine?' A fair question if posed by a curious little mind. The use of the word *kala* led to one inference: she had been introduced to the Fairometer. And if it wasn't her upbringing, when and how had colourism infiltrated her mind? Through enormous billboards and TV advertisements featuring Bollywood celebrities endorsing fairness creams? Through other children in school, picking up conversations around her? Were these to blame? Certainly not her innocent little mind. The list of influences was endless in my time, in the 1980s, and tragically the same list existed in 2019. In a few more years, she would be introduced to social media; the combined influences would be ineluctable.

Dumbfounded, I didn't have an answer for her. 'I've tanned a lot from a beach holiday,' I replied, stooping in my own eyes for not enlightening her with prejudice-free ideologies. Her question, along with the two preceding run-ins with colourism, fired two shots simultaneously.

It brought horrific childhood memories to the forefront again, together with the realisation that my little niece would also be unable to whitewash the dark imprints of colourism. Her clean and uncorrupted mind was now subconsciously building a lie that I had lived through for decades. I felt sorry for her.

The next morning, I headed to Karol Bagh, excited to visit my extended family and refresh my childhood memories. As I walked down the narrow alley to Nani's house, I saw a familiar face walking in my direction, a childhood friend, Aarti. We frequently played *gilli-danda* in the alley. Although Aarti always beat me, a warm feeling came over me as soon as I saw her. Her dexterity when it came to catching the *gilli* never failed her. I wondered who would win if we played right this moment. Aarti had put on several stones; her face was still the same, brown birthmark on her left cheek and chestnut brown eyes. She didn't seem to recognise me, though. I waved at her. She didn't react.

'Hi Aarti, it's me, Shweta. Remember me?' I said, wearing a big grin when we were less than a meter apart. She stared at me, her eyes examining me, working very hard to recall our relationship. 'We used to play *gilli-danda* here. Remember?' I said, dropping more reminders. She still couldn't place me.

'Shweta...from Japan.' I tried one last time, almost wondering if I had mistaken a stranger for Aarti.

'Oh my God, you! I didn't recognise you, Shweta. Your curly hair and your colour – what happened? I thought a Black woman was approaching me,' she said. I was stunned by her words, speechless for several seconds.

'What's wrong with looking like a Black woman?!' I asked, infuriated.

'Um, nothing. I...I didn't mean that. I didn't mean it *like* that.'

'I think you did.'

I was used to colourist comments from people of the previous generation, set in their ways. My niece's question surprised me, but I understood it wasn't her; it was an innocent child's observation with words put in her mouth by society. But this remark from someone of my generation stunned, disappointed, and angered me. It's because this was both a colourist and a racist remark.

I walked off with nothing more to say, concealing one more emotion I refused to acknowledge in my own head.

If change is the only constant, then why does history repeat itself? Over three decades, nothing had changed when it came to systemic colourism, manifested in mindsets from birth. History was repeating itself more and more fiercely, colourism being more rampant than ever. But then again, who was I to judge when I hadn't changed either? So, I suppressed my story then too. The vessel of tolerance wasn't full to the brim yet.

I was still using the cream secretly, albeit infrequently, until George Floyd's death in May 2020. The video clip taken by a passer-by recording the atrocity went viral. A black man's life had been taken prematurely by a white police officer for, let's be honest, being black. The Black Lives Matter protests spread like wildfire from major cities in the US to cultural capitals around the world, including London.

I attended one protest with my family in our local park on 20 June 2020. Kareena and Rohan passionately created posters to show their support: one with a black fist and the other with names of countless black lives lost to racism in recent years. I sat on the grass, listening intently and cheering for people sharing their experiences of racism. White supremacy and oppression of certain races appalled me like never before. Of course, I had studied heart-breaking historic events in school - slavery, Apartheid in South Africa, and the colonisation of India - but sadly, as a human race, we only tend to learn when we have gone through a horrific experience in our own time. It was when an incident came close to home, and on a global scale, that my inner self awakened. The protest in my local park hit the bullseye. Hard. At the end of the protest, I approached a middle-aged black man to commend him for sharing his stories. As I nodded along in sympathy, I reached for my red tennis cap, adjusting it to prevent my face from tanning. It was at that exact moment when my eyes left his face and never found the courage to return. Guilt consumed me.

I was reminded of my interaction with Aarti. You're not going to like me as I'm about to reveal the emotion her words invoked.

I felt offended.

With the 'fair is beautiful' narrative drummed into me from the age of six, I was offended when I was told I look like a black woman. That day, I recognised that not wanting to look like someone, their appearance being the first thing we judge, is the genesis of racism. I had become a colourist when I gave in to colourism. Having claimed to myself that I am not a racist, that day I realised that anti-Blackness manifests in subtle ways because of this narrative. That my reaction was no different to Aarti's words.

I sheepishly told the Black man that my family is waiting for me and wrapped up the conversation. Feeling ashamed, I spent the entire walk back home wondering how I got to this stage, unpacking colourism in my head.

It's difficult to pinpoint the exact origin of colourism in India given the country was conquered by several rulers with a lighter skin tone – Aryans, Mughals, British, and Portuguese to name a few – over millennia. In addition to this, India's caste and class stratification, which originated in ancient times, is still a prevalent social construct. What's most

241

perplexing, though, are glimpses of colourism in the Hindu pantheon, specifically in the depictions of Lord Krishna and Goddess Kali. Ancient texts did mention the colour of gods and goddesses but without a prejudicial undertone. So, when did society begin to inflict prejudice in the depiction of the divine? Why was Krishna, a black-skinned male god, depicted as people pleased – mostly fair-skinned – and Kali, a black-skinned goddess, depicted only in black? One could go around in circles pursuing an answer.

I wondered how much India's last colonisation by the British Empire, which brought with it ideologies of white supremacy and white skin privilege, exacerbated colourism. 'Black Indians' or 'Darkies' were denied entry into restaurants and educational institutions during the British Raj. Light-skinned Indians were hired for odd jobs more frequently than those with darker skin.

Since then, colourism spread like the plague in India and the country opted for herd immunity: let every single Indian catch it, become obsessed with the 'fair is beautiful' and 'fair is successful' notions, work tirelessly on becoming fairer, and grow immune to colourist comments. I wasn't spared by this virus either. Manufacturers of skin care products, seeing the virus thrive, invented fairness creams as a 'cure'. A carefully planned, addictive cure with images of women in four different shades of the Fairometer.

Just a little fairer and then I'll stop, I had told myself for years. But how fair was fair enough? More importantly, why did I let it matter? If I was to continue striving for a higher reading on the Fairometer, not appreciating my natural colour, I had no right to participate in a protest speaking up for people darker than me.

This realisation forced me to revisit my daily 'little

wrong' of applying skin-whitening creams, an act of waving the white flag in front of colourism. But this daily act had accumulated into a 'big wrong': implicitly encouraging colourism and validating white skin privilege. This felt more like joining forces. It was this realisation, the subtle but important difference between the two, that was the last drop in the vessel of tolerance. It was my guilt about joining forces that caused the spillage.

The process of unlearning thirty-eight years of colourism was far more challenging than I had envisaged, similar to that of an addict getting clean. Sounds simple: dispose of the creams, tell yourself you're beautiful, and embrace the sun. The number of times I have wanted to purchase that cream again. The number of times I have felt unpretty when I heard comments describing other women as 'fair and beautiful'. The number of times I have wanted to seek shade when I dared step out in the sun.

'You've tanned,' smiled Amit, months into my reformation. I frowned instinctively because I still was struggling with the unlearning, missing the point that it was a compliment. Another few months later, during a holiday in August 2021, I reluctantly joined Rohan and Kareena, now twelve and fourteen, in an aqua park on the beach. There was nowhere to hide. Every sunray touching my skin felt like the prick of a needle. As I held Rohan and Kareena's hands, standing on an inflatable mountain three meters high, they both said, 'We know how hard this is for you. We're proud of you, Mummy.' I looked into their eyes, and I knew they weren't referring to the drop in front of us. I had come clean to my children, admitting that I continued to use the cream until 2020. They knew I was still battling against my instinct to stay out of the sun.

We jumped, with me taking the lead. We climbed up that inflatable again and jumped again. And again. And again. On every drop, in the moments when I was suspended in the air, plunging towards the bed of water, I felt shame and pride. Shame for denying my children and myself this joy and connection until now. Pride for finally embracing my colour and the sun. I also used this opportunity to obliterate all the nicknames etched in my mind. Bedwetter, Susu Shweta, The Ugly Duckling, Beggar's Child, Kallo, Blackie, and Bastard – one splash at a time, every nickname was erased like writing in the sand washed away by a wave. That day, I grew closer to my children. That day, I realised that in my quest for belonging, I had wandered so far off the path that I no longer belonged to myself. Nor to my beliefs that a person's virtues are all that matters, not their colour. I had abandoned the fight I had wanted to put up against colourism all my life.

It was high time I ditched my complex instead. And eighteen months since I did, all the darkness within is gone. I now feel fair in the true sense. I did it. At age forty-five, I am now clean. Cleansed of the cream, the complex, and all colour prejudice.

I belong to myself and am proud to be The Black Rose.

Epilogue

The Black Rose is my personal fight against colourism, of which I was both a victim and a perpetrator. A victim because of the societal pressure I endured, being at the bottom end of the Fairometer. A culprit, in my own eyes, because instead of fighting it, I succumbed. Just like millions of other women in India secretly going through the same struggle daily, I also joined the fairness race, one minute determined to change perceptions and the next minute, applying fairness creams.

As I started writing, I didn't just open my own Pandora's Box, I discovered alarming facts about colourism globally. I learned that this is not just my story, it's over a billion – that's right, a billion – buried stories and this is how.

- More than 50% of all skincare products sold in India are to lighten the skin.

- In East Asian culture, women prefer a fairer skin tone because they believe in an old saying: *A white complexion covers seven flaws*. China alone boasted sales of 440 billion yuan in 2019 from skin-whitening products.

- $2.3 billion was spent in the US on such products in 2020.

I could go on with staggering statistics from Latin

America, the Middle East and the whole of Africa, but you get the drift. In short, a significant proportion of the non-white world – essentially half the world – aspires to be fairer. Am I wrong in concluding that colourism affects billions when light skin is seen as the pinnacle of beauty? And success? Reaching out for whitening creams to attain lighter skin starts with one comment usually at a young age: 'You're too dark.'

Creams are just the tip of the iceberg. There is an even darker side to the flourishing skin-whitening industry: injectables and bleaching agents with harmful long-term effects. Chemicals such as mercury, hydroquinone, and tretinoin – which have been reported to have links to gastric irritation, liver and kidney damage, blood poisoning, cancer, and complications during pregnancy, to name a few – continue to be used in many cosmetic products despite many countries declaring their use illegal. Speaking of pregnancy, there have been numerous articles about women bleaching their babies. Some expectant mothers even take bleaching pills to lighten the skin of their unborn babies! Last but not the least, a plethora of whitening products are available to lighten intimate parts of the body – vaginal and anal areas. Need I say more?

The global skin-whitening market, valued at US $8.6 billion in 2020, is estimated to reach $12.3 billion by 2027.[5] Things are changing rapidly. For the worse. Colourism is spreading like a silent global pandemic because the astronomical growth in the skin-whitening industry is driven by two deeply entrenched narratives: *fair is beautiful* and *fair is successful*.

I feel empowered in discovering many other anti-colourism activists working tirelessly to dismantle these narratives daily and highly recommend the following individuals and organisations as a great place to start your healing journey. I started mine here.

- **Dark is Beautiful** is an Indian non-profit awareness and advocacy campaign that exists to fight colourism. Over the last 12 years, it has successfully drawn attention to the unjust effects of skin-colour bias in India and worldwide. Through events and workshops, the organisation tells people that their value and self-worth do not depend on the colour of their skin.

  Facebook: @darkisbeautiful

  Instagram: @darkisbeautifulcampaign

  Website: www.darkisbeautiful.in

- **Dr Sarah L. Webb** is an international speaker, consultant, and coach. She launched the global initiative **Colorism Healing** in 2013 to raise critical awareness about colourism and foster individual and collective healing through creative and critical work.

  Instagram: @colorismhealing

  TikTok: @colorismhealing

  Website: www.colorismhealing.com

- **Swarnaa Rajalingam** is a Sydney-based South Asian content creator who uses her platform to spark dialogue on issues that are close to her heart. This includes but is not limited to colourism, the need for representation, body positivity, disability awareness and mental health issues.

  Instagram: @thelifeofasocialbutterfly

Tiktok: @tloasbutterfly

- **Anita Kalathara** is an actress, voice-over artist and writer. She's outspoken about her experiences of colourism, which led her to write, produce and star in the short film, *Unfair & Lovely* to expose the issues that colourism has created. The film went viral on YouTube and has been played in festivals across the US. She continues to speak against colourism via social media and features on podcasts regularly.

Instagram: @anitakalathara

TikTok: @anitakalathara

YouTube: @anitabeme

Thank you to all the readers whose hands this book reaches. I am sorry if my story has resonated with you and brought back unpleasant memories of your own experiences. I am here to support you in any way I can. To those readers unaware of the detrimental impact of colourism, I hope *The Black Rose* was a thought-provoking read.

ACKNOWLEDGEMENTS

I would like to start by thanking my husband, Amit, for encouraging me to continue writing after I penned my prologue on a park bench and shared it with him. Thank you to my mother, Veena, and brother, Neeraj, for reliving my story with me, for their patience through umpteen phone calls to verify information, and for their support. I know learning some of my buried secrets was painful for them too. Thank you to my two teenagers, Kareen and Rohan, for putting up with me the entire year while I was consumed by the writing process. And for also being my first beta-readers, chapter by chapter. There's nothing like your children's brutal honesty to keep you rewriting! Friends Jane, Shalini, Vani, Elizabeth, Sonia, Aliya, Priya, Kaushika and many others, thank you for reading sections of or the entire manuscript, for providing me with vital feedback, and for giving me the strength to persevere. Finally, the biggest thank you to my editors, Noo Sara-Wiwa and Shweta Ganesh Kumar for their developmental edits, Hannah Boursnell for copy editing, and Tatiana Wilde for the final proofreading. Your professional feedback has helped me refine my narration.

ABOUT THE AUTHOR

Shweta Aggarwal is an anti-colourism activist with a colourful life. A computer science engineer by way of background, her passion is dance and writing. After moving to London in 2000, she ran a Bollywood dance company, Threebee (Bold, Beautiful and very Bollywood), alongside working at UBS in their IT department. As the creative director of the company for 10 years, some proud moments include her troupe featuring as a semi-finalist in *Britain's Got Talent* 2010 and being invited by the London Olympics team to audition for the closing ceremony in 2012.

A new passion emerged when she wrapped up the dance company to prioritise family life. The lack of representation in children's books inspired Shweta to launch the Dev and Ollie series of picture books based on festivals in India. The books are popular in schools and libraries all over the world. Shweta was awarded the Asian Women of Achievement Award for Arts & Culture in 2016 and invited by the late Her Majesty the Queen to Buckingham Palace for the UK-India Year of Culture in 2017. In 2020, triggered by the Black Lives Matter movement, Shweta started writing her memoir based on her journey through colourism from the age of six. Shweta's mission is simple: to instigate change, for which she is prepared to risk exposing herself to the world.

shwetaaggarwal.com

Instagram | Facebook | TikTok: @theblackroseway

References & Further Reading

1   'New words list June 2015' (online), Oxford English Dictionary, https://public.oed.com/updates/new-words-list-june-2015/ (June 2015)

2   'How George Floyd Was Killed in Police Custody' (online) by Evan Hill, Ainara Tiefenthäler, Christiaan Triebert, Drew Jordan, Haley Willis and Robin Stein https://www.nytimes.com/2020/05/31/us/george-floyd-investigation.html (31 May 2020)

3   Assassination of Indira Gandhi (online), Wikipedia, https://en.wikipedia.org/wiki/Assassination_of_Indira_Gandhi

4   Great Hanshin Earthquake (online), Britannica https://www.britannica.com/event/Kobe-earthquake-of-1995

5   'The Dark Side of Skin Lightening' (online) by Vicky Feng and David Rovella at Bloomberg. https://www.bloomberg.com/news/articles/2021-09-17/why-skin-lightening-is-big-business-in-some-parts-of-the-world (17 September 2021)

Made in United States
North Haven, CT
17 January 2023

31181560R00157

Made in United States
Orlando, FL
26 May 2022